Nothing Stays the Same Forever

NOTHING STAYS THE SAME FOREVER

By Gail Radley

Crown Publishers, Inc. New York

Published by Crown Publishers, Inc., 225 Park Avenue South, New York, New
York 10003 and represented in Canada by the Canadian MANDA Group.
CROWN is a trademark of Crown Publishers, Inc.
Manufactured in the United States of America

Library of Congress Cataloging-in-Publication Data

Radley, Gail. Nothing stays the same forever.
    Summary: Twelve-year-old Carrie, who wants to be an artist, is concerned
about her widowed father's upcoming marriage and the future of an elderly
friend.
    [1. Fathers and daughters—Fiction, 2. Remarriage—Fiction.
3. Old age—Fiction]
I. Title. PZ7.R1223 No.   1981   [Fic]   81-12515   AACR2

ISBN 0-517-56876-4

10 9 8 7 6 5 4 3 2 1

First Crown Paperback Edition, 1988

For my husband, Joe Killeen,
who nurtured the dream. Thank you.

NOTHING STAYS THE SAME FOREVER

CHAPTER
1

I lingered by my father's doorway, watching him get ready for his date and trying to think of some subtle yet pointed things to say. Something that would make him want to tell me just what was going on between him and Sharon.

Dad put the points of his collar under his sports jacket, then pulled them out again and studied them in the mirror.

"Where are you going tonight?" I asked, hoping it wasn't some romantic hideaway couples are always going to in the movies. Just thinking that Dad might be half of a couple made me cringe.

"I don't know yet. Sharon is going to surprise me. Think the collar is supposed to go in or out?"

"How 'bout one of each? Then you'd be half right, anyway."

He looked at me and laughed. "Thanks a lot. Out, I think."

He took so much care with how he looked when he went out with Sharon. He didn't dress for work this way. He just put on his clothes and left. I grasped for some way to destroy the careful image he was building.

"Does it really matter? Will she give you an *F* for the evening if you're not dressed right?"

He laughed again. "A gentleman likes to be well dressed when he calls on a lady," he said.

I'd met Sharon briefly a couple of times. She was as tall as Dad, but blond and freckled. She didn't look a thing like Mom, and I couldn't imagine why Dad was attracted to her.

I laid one bare foot on top of the other and leaned against the doorframe. My feet had pale crisscross lines from walking to and from school in sandals. But now that school was out, those lines would soon become as tanned as the rest of my feet. "It's too hot to wear a jacket," I said.

"Well, one should be prepared."

Then he started fussing with his hair. Dad had kept a crew cut long after most fathers had let theirs grow out. He had a boyish face and the crew cut almost looked good. But since he had met Sharon, his hair was beginning to bush out.

Everything seemed to be quietly changing. Not just Dad's looks, but our whole life. I was used to my sister, Phyllis, going out. She was eighteen and had gone out with her boyfriend, Al, every Saturday night since she was fourteen. Dad and I would watch the Saturday night movie or play checkers. He always said he did enough running around in fancy clothes during the week and that he just wanted to relax at home with me. But when Sharon came into his life, everything changed. Oh, he had had dates before, but not week after week with the same woman. The other times hadn't seemed important enough to worry about. Now Sharon's name popped up in nearly every conversation. I didn't like it one bit.

I was thinking of asking him what Mom would think if she were still alive when Phyllis walked into the room, modeling her new pants suit.

"How do you like it?" she asked.

"It has stripes," I observed. It was all I could think of to say.

"Vertical stripes are supposed to be slimming," she said.

"Right." I couldn't help thinking that all it did was make her look like a barrel. Phyllis is one of those people who talk about dieting over spaghetti and spumoni.

Dad said, "You look lovely, Phyllis. Red is a nice color on you." He gave me a look that meant "Be nice."

"So where are you and Al going tonight?"

"To the movies." She turned to Dad. "Are you sure it's all right for Carrie and Bridget to be alone tonight? I could still call Marsha—she said she'd cover for me."

"I don't need to be watched!"

Phyllis twisted her mouth into a sarcastic little

smirk. "Your friend Bridget is about as reliable as a paper umbrella in a thunderstorm. And *such* a good influence."

I once overheard Dad tell Phyllis that Bridget's parents were too liberal and that Bridget was growing up wild. Bridget is my best friend and she's not wild—just unique. "Since when are you the judge of my friends?" I demanded.

"Carrie," Dad broke in, "Phyllis is only concerned about you. And, Phyllis, I think Carrie is old enough to manage now. Besides, I'll be home early."

I didn't need that kind of concern from Phyllis. Being six years older than me, she thought I was a great one to boss around. She shrugged and left the room.

A moment later, a horn blew outside.

"I'm leaving, Dad!" yelled Phyllis, pounding down the stairs.

"Have fun!" he said.

Why she let her dumb boyfriend honk for her like she was a carhop at a drive-in restaurant, I'd never know. I asked her once and she just said that she and Al were "beyond those silly dating rules."

Dad tucked his wallet in his pocket and turned to me. "You going to be okay tonight, honey?"

For a moment I was startled by his appearance: the slim lines of his doe-colored trousers nearly matched the shade of his eyes; the points of his brown shirt, unbuttoned to the neck, stood crisply on his jacket lapels.

"Sure," I replied.

He glanced at his watch. "Shouldn't Bridget be here now?"

"She'll be along soon."

"You and Bridget be careful. Keep the doors locked. Bridget has some strange ideas at times, so put my mind at ease and have a quiet, uneventful evening."

"We will, Dad."

"Should I call over there?"

"To Bridget's? No. Stop worrying. I am twelve, after all. I can be alone for a minute without going to pieces."

He leaned over and kissed my forehead. "Of course you can. I just hate to leave you here alone, but I'm running late . . ."

"Go. It's okay, really." Maybe I didn't have to worry. Maybe the whole thing would blow over on its own.

He smiled. "If you need anything, Bridget's father will be at home. Mrs. Calloway is out leading a therapy group or something tonight."

"Right."

He gave my hair a playful tug, like he used to do when I was little, and was gone.

I waited until I heard the front door shut and then went to the window in my room and watched him stride out to the car. Suddenly I felt very lonely.

Dad stopped by the car, and I saw that Bridget was

coming. She had a knapsack on her back and a stack of records under her arm. He said something to her and then got in the car. I ran downstairs to let her in.

She grinned at me from beneath the red snap-down cap her father had given her. Bridget always wore a hat. It could be 105 degrees and Bridget would wear a hat. "Brian gave me a bunch of his old records," she announced.

Her sixteen-year-old brother was always giving her the remnants of his former interests. We spread the albums on the floor. "These aren't so old," I said. "Why'd he give you these?"

"They're all hard rock. He says they rattle his brain. He's listening to soft rock and country now." She pulled four records out of their covers and stacked them onto the stereo. "You're lucky," she said, "getting the house to yourself like this. Between my mom, my dad and my brother, somebody's always around. They never seem to go out at the same time."

"Yeah, but your parents are interesting and your brother's not bossy like Phyllis."

"That's because Brian is always too busy reading to be bossy," said Bridget. "My parents are always asking me questions and trying to understand me. It drives me up the wall sometimes."

Night in the Ruts dropped onto the turntable and the needle eased onto it. Bridget turned the volume way up and then pulled one of the sofa cushions onto the floor and lay back to listen to Aerosmith.

I settled down across from her, resting my feet on top of the sofa. It was true. Not long ago, Mr. Calloway, who taught sociology at Tulane University, sat Bridget and me down and asked us what we'd do about problems like unemployment, drugs and race relations.

"Why ask us?" I wondered.

Bridget answered for him. "He's gathering information so they can talk about it in his class."

Mr. Calloway sat forward in his chair. "I want to know the views of young people."

Mrs. Calloway heard us and slipped into the room. She listened for a short time; then she started asking us questions. "How would you feel if a close friend was on drugs?" "How would you feel if you were told you'd be bused to another school?" She was a social worker and had to understand people whether she wanted to or not.

We went along with them for a while, and then Bridget made some excuse to get us out of there. But even with all their questions, I thought Bridget was lucky to have two parents.

I'm not saying Dad wasn't a good parent. He loved Phyllis and me a lot and was always trying to show it by taking us places and spending time with us. He told me I could talk with him about anything, but whenever I brought up uncomfortable things, he got nervous. Mom had been the person I went to if I had a real problem, but she died of cancer when I was eight.

"Why did she have to die?" I used to ask. "She was

in the hospital a lot—why didn't they make her better?"

"These things happen," he would say in a low voice. "Cancer is . . . difficult."

Finally Phyllis had pulled me aside. "Stop asking him dumb questions. Can't you see it hurts him to talk about her? If you really want to know something, ask me."

She had waited expectantly. Phyllis, the honorary parent.

I'd frowned. "I just wish Mom was still here, that's all."

"Well, she's not, so you might as well face it," Phyllis had said.

I don't think Mom ever told me that I could talk to her about anything. Just the way she was—relaxed and interested—made me want to talk.

The music throbbed through the house. I could feel the floor vibrating. It was nice to have the house to ourselves. No one would lecture us about being considerate.

I opened a bag of pretzels, took a handful and pushed them toward Bridget. "Pretzels!" I hollered.

She opened her eyes and blinked at me as if she were returning from a faraway place. I pointed to the bag. She rolled over, brushed the hair away from her face and took a pretzel.

"My uncle Greg wrote me the other day," she shouted.

"Who?" I shouted back.

"Uncle Greg! The artist in New York!"

"Oh!" The heavy, persistent drumming made it nearly impossible to sit still. I concentrated all my energy onto my tapping foot, but I really felt like dancing.

Bridget got up and cut the volume back. She sat down on the cushion. "He told me about an art workshop that will be given this August in the Adirondacks. He went to it when he was a kid. He said it was better than any art class he ever had." Bridget pulled a pamphlet out of her back pocket and spread it out on the floor. "Look at this. Painting, pen-and-ink drawing, all kinds of sculpture . . ."

It looked fantastic. They taught every kind of art I could think of. And all the instructors were working artists, not just teachers. There was a picture of where it would be held—a collection of small A-frame buildings sprinkled over rolling green hills. It looked like a place that could bring art out of a turnip. The price was incredible, too. Two hundred dollars for two weeks. And that didn't include getting there.

"Can you imagine how much we'd learn, studying art all day for two weeks? Surrounded by people who are already successful?" Bridget asked. "We'd become super artists!"

I nodded, studying the pamphlet. Bridget really wanted to be an artist. I guess that was one reason we were best friends. Lots of kids wanted to be something different each week, but Bridget and I had wanted to be artists as long as we could remember.

"And if that's not enough," she went on, "Uncle Greg will take us to New York City after the workshop and show us around."

"Us?"

She grinned, "Yeah! I called him as soon as the letter arrived. I told him about you and asked if you could come. He said, 'Sure.' You're going to love him, Carrie. He's terrific."

"It sounds great. I don't know if Dad'll go for this or not. I've never been outside of Louisiana, let alone all the way to New York by myself."

"You won't be alone. I'll be with you."

That, I knew, would not reassure Dad. Ever since that Saturday when he found Bridget and me marching in a jazz funeral for someone we didn't even know, he had taken a somewhat dim view of Bridget. "You know what I mean," I said aloud.

"Yeah. Well, just tell him that artists need to travel."

"Maybe so." Summer had already begun and I didn't have any special plans. Dad wasn't even taking us on vacation this year. That was another change that riled me. We always went on vacation. It was one of the few things we managed to do as a family, and I always looked forward to it. Usually we stayed in a motel along the Gulf of Mexico and swam. Sometimes we'd stop at the Art Center in Lafayette because Dad knew I liked to see the exhibits. One time we stayed at the Hot Wells Health Resort and swam in mineral water that was 113 degrees!

Dad had said he couldn't take the time away from work this year, but I was sure he didn't want to leave Sharon. There was no reason why I couldn't have a vacation with Bridget, though. Dad would probably be too busy with Sharon to miss me, and if I was at the workshop he wouldn't have to worry about me when he went out. Maybe that would help convince him.

Bridget tossed me the pretzel bag and stood up. "I'm starved. Have you got any ice cream?"

"Yeah. Come on."

We went into the kitchen, and Bridget took out the ice cream and bowls. I climbed up on the stool and began looking in the cupboards. I knew Phyllis had stashed chocolate syrup, nuts, whip-cream mix and cherries behind the soup and macaroni. (More than once, I'd caught her gorging herself late at night.) Bridget and I made great sloppy sundaes. Bridget used so many cherries hers looked like a chocolate cherry bush.

Then we watched a movie on TV about a fourteen-year-old girl who was being held prisoner in a cave by an apelike creature. He had snatched her out of her house one night when she was there alone. Every night the creature brought another kid to the cave, and they were all terrified of what he might do. The movie made the hair on the back of my neck prickle. I looked at Bridget. She was pushing cherries through the syrup and melted ice cream in her bowl and then licking them. She didn't look bothered at all.

I got up and checked the locks on all the doors. I sat down for five minutes more and then got up again and stretched.

"I'm getting tired of TV," I said. "Let's do something else."

Bridget popped another cherry into her mouth and turned off the set. "It's a sappy movie anyhow," she said. "You know how it ends?"

"How?" I asked, although I wasn't sure I wanted to know.

"The girl wakes up and finds it's all a dream."

"Really?"

"Yeah. I read the book."

We thumbed through Dad's *New Yorker* magazines, looking at the cartoons. Some of them were super. I hoped I'd be able to draw that well someday.

Then Bridget said, "Let's rearrange the living-room furniture."

"That's a great idea. This room has looked the same for years."

"My mom's always rearranging our furniture. She says a creative environment encourages creative thinking."

"My mom used to change our living room around a lot, too," I said. She was always bringing some special little thing home with her—a stained-glass ornament for the kitchen window, a vase for the living room. She knew how to move a few lamps and change the whole atmosphere in a room. I looked at the stack of newspapers on the coffee table.

"The first thing to do is to get rid of these," I said, picking up an armload.

"Right." Bridget gathered up the rest.

After we carried the papers down to the basement, we looked around the room.

"You have very nice furniture," said Bridget pensively, "but it's placed all wrong."

"I know. Phyllis and Dad have no flair for decorating. They just do what's practical."

We began to push the furniture around, trying to see where pieces would look best. We finally ended up with the sofa beneath the stairs so it faced the bay window. We put the two big avocado trees at each end of the sofa. Dad's easy chair, which was getting ratty-looking, was pushed into a shadowy corner. The coffee table was sturdy, so we put cushions and an extra bedspread on it and turned it into a window seat.

Decorating made me happy. I remembered coming home from school when I was six and finding Mom had changed everything around. I had loved that. It was almost like being in a new house.

Maybe when Dad saw our decorating job he'd remember that, I thought. The new environment might even make him feel like staying home more. I could rearrange the furniture from time to time, just like Mom had. We had just taken Dad's old college textbooks off the shelf when the front door swung open and he walked in.

"Hi," he said. "What are you doing with the books?"

"Taking them to your room. The bookshelf looked jammed, and you never read these anyway."

"I see." He looked around the room and rubbed the bridge of his nose with two fingers.

"Do you like the new room?"

"It's—interesting. Different."

He sat down on the sofa. The overhanging branches of the avocado trees brushed his head. He leaned forward to get out from under them, and Bridget and I exchanged glances.

"That didn't happen when we sat there," I said.

"Well, perhaps the arrangement needs a little more thought," he replied gently.

"We can move the pots back a little until the plants are taller," Bridget suggested.

"Dad, do you know where that box with the little statues and vases is? We thought we'd put them on the bookshelf."

Dad rose and took off his sports jacket. "Listen, do you girls think you could restrain yourselves until morning? It's nearly midnight."

"Oh. Sure, Dad," I said. "I think we could."

"Well, good night, then."

"Good night," we chorused.

* * *

We slept on mattresses on the floor side by side. I awoke to see the early morning sun slanting in through the window. Bridget moaned softly and pulled the sheet over her head, turning herself into a softly breathing white lump.

I lay on my back, looking at the sunlight through half-closed eyelids. I thought of the decorating job Bridget and I had done. We had taken an ordinary, nondescript living room and given it atmosphere. I had thought Dad would be impressed, but he didn't seem to be. Maybe he was still thinking about his date with Sharon.

I wondered what Dad did on a date. Dance and drink wine at a nightclub? Go to the movies? And what did they talk about? The office? Me and Phyllis? Did he tell her stories of the stupid things I did when I was little? Did they sit there laughing at me? I wondered what she had done to make Dad care about her so much.

Dad's infatuation didn't seem to be bothering Phyllis. She wasn't home much anyway. She worked at a nursing home and most evenings she was with Al or out shopping. She probably hadn't even noticed all the changes or the fact that Dad couldn't stop talking about Sharon.

The aroma of fresh coffee seeped into the room, and I realized Dad and Phyllis must be starting breakfast. I nudged the white lump.

"Uh," it said.

I shook it again. "Time to get up," I said.

A mass of hair slowly emerged from beneath the sheet and then a face. "Is it morning?"

"Yup. Let's go eat."

I put on my cutoffs and T-shirt and started brushing my hair while Bridget struggled to her feet and began to dress. From her knapsack she extracted a very short pair of cutoffs and a lavender peasant blouse with lace sleeves. To this she added a pair of red suspenders, and then she began hunting around for her red cap.

For one traitorous moment, I wished she could look like everyone else, if only for this one morning, so she could walk into the kitchen and Dad would think, "Now, there is a good, average, all-American kid—the perfect one to go with Carrie to New York this summer." But I knew what Dad would think—"Weird!"

"Something interesting I've noticed," Dad had said to me once. "Phyllis picks friends like herself— steady, down-to-earth girls. You picked Bridget—an opposite."

"Bridget and I aren't opposites."

"You're both girls and you both like art. There it ends."

"No, Dad, we have lots in common."

"Look at the way she dresses, the things she likes to do. Whether you want to see it or not, Carrie, you're more like your sister."

You wish I was, I had thought to myself. Though he'd said it politely, I knew it was a dig at Bridget, and it made me mad. Why couldn't Dad appreciate her for who she was? It would be unfair to ask her to change. That'd be like asking the Mississippi River not to flow into the Gulf or asking Michelangelo to paint a bathroom brainwash gray.

"Have you seen my cap?" Bridget asked.

"On the chair."

We went down to the kitchen. Only Dad was there; Phyllis was still in bed. He peered at us from over his magazine. "Good morning, girls." Then he stared at Bridget. "You certainly are an eyeful."

"Thanks," said Bridget, smiling. She took most everything as a compliment. I was glad she didn't realize how Dad really felt.

"Did you have a good time last night?" I asked.

"Yes, thanks."

"Where'd you go?"

"Dinner and a play."

"You got home before Phyllis."

"If I'd been much later I might not have recognized the house."

I glanced at him out of the corner of my eye. I wondered if he was hoping we would put everything back. Maybe he looked for practicality more than mood in a living room. But he didn't say any more. "Bridget, I'm gonna fry an egg. You want one?"

"Egg? No, thanks, not in the morning. I can't stand that yellow eye ogling me at this hour. Do you have any tangerines?"

"Sure. Help yourself."

Bridget disappeared into the refrigerator. I cracked an egg into the skillet, looked over Dad's shoulder and saw that he was reading *Sports Illustrated.* "Since when are you interested in sports?" I asked.

He smiled up at me. "Sharon's quite a sports enthusiast. I thought it was about time to round out that part of my personality."

"I'll loan you some of my art books if you don't feel round enough."

"What? Oh no, that's all right, Carrie. I played some baseball in high school, you know, but it's been years . . . Sharon jogs and she's going to teach me soon."

Bridget had found her tangerine and was busily separating the sections and pulling off the little white strings that clung to them. "My brother read *The Zen of Running.*"

Dad looked up. "He jogs?"

"No, he never got to the actual running."

Dad just looked at her.

"Brian reads everything, but he hardly does anything." She laid another string onto her little pile and looked at it with interest. "You know, I never really looked at these things before. They're like vines, but they have their own texture. Maybe I'll do a painting of them magnified a thousand times."

Dad raised one eyebrow and returned to his magazine.

After breakfast, Bridget gathered up her things and went home.

Phyllis padded into the kitchen like a bear unwillingly coming out of hibernation and began to make breakfast.

Dad had disappeared. I found him in front of his mirror, gently prodding the creases in his forehead and the crinkly lines around his eyes. He looked startled. "I didn't hear you come in," he said. "Give me your honest opinion. Do you think I'm looking older?"

I sat down on the bed. "Older than what? Not older than a father."

"Well, people always thought I looked younger than I am. I'm beginning to think that's changed."

"Your hair's longer."

"I thought it might help."

"Dad, you look like yourself," I said. "I don't think you should change, ever."

"Thanks, honey. What's on your mind today, anyway?"

I pulled out the pamphlet Bridget had left with me. "Bridget's going to an art workshop. I wondered if I could go, too."

Dad studied the pamphlet in his agonizingly slow way, reading every little word. Finally he handed it back to me. "I don't think so, honey."

Be calm, I told myself. Reason with him. "Why not? We don't have anything special going on this summer."

"Oh, I wouldn't say that. It's going to be a very special summer."

"Why?"

He started to smile. "Oh, we'll be doing things with Sharon," he said vaguely.

"Well, that's great for you," I said. "But I'd like to do something this summer, too."

"I'd like you and Sharon to get to know each other."

"Dad, I know her. I've met her a couple of times. Besides, she's interested in you, not me—"

"Oh, she wants to get to know you, too. We'll be going places, doing things. Maybe Lake Pontchartrain Amusement Park."

I grimaced. "Who cares about an amusement park when I can go to this workshop? It's important to me. And it's only two weeks. Besides, Bridget's uncle Greg is an artist, and he's going to show us around New York City. I might not get another chance like this."

"It's just not the time. I don't want you to go all the way to New York with Bridget," Dad said. "Besides, it'd be well over two hundred dollars. Phyllis's college is coming up soon. We can't afford any extra expenses."

"What if I earn the money?" I suggested. "I could work. I could earn the money myself. How 'bout that?"

Dad drew his eyebrows together. "I suppose that might change things some, although I'd prefer to have you home. But you'd never—"

"It doesn't start till August 13th. That's almost two months," I said. "I can do it. Wait and see." I hurried away before he could think of another reason to say no.

CHAPTER
2

I started out my moneymaking efforts by advertising. That morning I made up a batch of cards with my name, age and phone number, stating that I wanted to do odd jobs. I posted these around the shopping center.

I put up a sign in my room: EARN $ FOR ART WORKSHOP. I planned to start talking with the neighbors on Monday morning.

I had never tried to earn that much money before, but I thought if I kept my mind on it, I could do it. I figure if you want something bad enough, you can make it happen.

That evening showed signs of being a pleasant one. Phyllis made lasagna, which was the best thing she cooked. Then Dad and I walked down to the store to buy Italian ices. We used to walk to the store after dinner all the time. Sometimes Phyllis would come, too. But Dad seldom had time for it anymore.

It was my favorite time for a walk. The street was quiet. In some of the houses I could see families gathered around their dinner tables.

"The years are slipping by so quickly," Dad said as we walked along. "Phyllis will be off to college soon and you're practically a teen-ager."

Usually I get tired of people telling me how much I've grown, but this time I laughed. I raised my arms like I did when I was a little girl and said, "Yup. I'm so-o big!"

Dad laughed at that and put his arm around me. It gave me a warm feeling inside.

When we got back from the store, we all settled down in front of the TV to watch Disney and eat dessert. *Super Dad* was on, a funny movie Dad had taken me to when I was younger.

Not fifteen minutes had passed when the telephone rang. Dad sprang out of his seat. Smiling, he settled into the easy chair, which had been moved back to its place beside the phone. He looked like he was planning on a long conversation. It had to be Sharon.

The movie was half over before he hung up the phone. Instead of coming back to finish it, he headed for his room.

"Where are you going?" I asked.

"To Sharon's. There's a sports special coming up on TV."

"But what about *Super Dad*?"

"I'm going to pass, honey. I've seen it before."

"You can watch the sports special here. I'll even make popcorn."

"Thanks, Carrie, but I just told Sharon I'd be over. Another time, okay? Phyllis, you going to be home?"

"Yes."

Then the phone rang again and Phyllis picked it up. "It's Al," she said.

Dad bounded up the stairs and I lay down on the couch, jiggling the avocado leaves with my big toe. Everybody was so busy.

A few minutes later, Dad returned, clean-shaven and in fresh clothes.

"Dad, can I invite Bridget over?"

"Carrie, how come you never spend time with the girls from your class?" he asked.

Bridget is a year older than I am and Dad acts like we're different generations. "Because *Bridget* is my best friend," I explained. "Can I?"

"No, not tonight. Phyllis will be here. A good chance for you girls to spend some time together." He gave me a kiss as he passed by. "Don't stay up late."

I sat scowling at the movie for five more minutes. Suddenly it seemed dumb and pointless. Phyllis was still talking to Al and showed no signs of stopping. I turned off the TV and went to bed early.

On Monday Bridget caught me by surprise. I had slept through breakfast and was having cereal for lunch. Bridget poked her head in the kitchen door just as I tipped the cereal bowl to my mouth to drain the last bit of milk.

She made a face. "Very uncouth," she said.

I laughed and set the bowl down. "What's up?"

Bridget pulled her floppy green hat down low over her eyes. "I'm going to the French Quarter."

"By yourself?"

"Only if you don't go."

I hated to tell her my dad wouldn't want me to go. I had heard him say often enough that it was a rough neighborhood, full of bars. Phyllis said there were a lot of bums hanging around and that it was dangerous when the sailors were in town. She and Al wouldn't even go there then. Still, I felt like a baby not being able to do something that Bridget felt so free to do. "I can't," I said. "I have to earn money for the workshop."

"Your dad's letting you go?" she asked, brightening.

"Not exactly." I sighed. "He said it's too much money. And he'd prefer I was home."

"Why?"

"He wants me to get to know Sharon and have 'fun' with them."

Bridget gave me a sympathetic look. "All summer?"

"It beats me. A day would be too much for me."

"Maybe it'll fizzle out," Bridget suggested cheerfully. "If it got serious, you'd be a stepfamily, and my mom says they have lots of problems. She probably won't want to get involved."

"I hope so. Dad did say if I could come up with the money myself, he might consider letting me go."

She frowned. "Two hundred dollars by August?"

"I know. But I've got to try."

"Well, come to the Quarter with me and maybe we can figure something out," Bridget said.

I sat the bowl in the sink and wiped my mouth on the dish towel hanging from the refrigerator. "No, I'm going to see if Mrs. Stebbins has work for me." Mrs. Stebbins was a white-haired lady of about seventy who lived two doors down from me. I didn't know her well, but she seemed nice. I also thought that since she lived alone, she might need some help.

"I've got to start earning that money fast," I said. "I have to get away from here for a while. My dad's so crazy about Sharon that I think he'd stand on his ear if she told him to. Everything's changing."

"It sounds terrible."

"But if I go to New York, maybe the thing will fizzle out by the time I get back. At least I won't have to sit home and hear Dad talk about her all the time."

"I don't blame you. Well, good luck with Mrs. Stebbins. I've got to get going."

"Okay. So long."

The screen door swung shut and Bridget was gone. I wouldn't be able to hang around with her for the next couple of months. I'd be too busy working. I felt a brief twinge of envy. But then I imagined myself with a fist-ful of money saying, "See, Dad, I did it!" and the envy vanished.

I went to the bathroom and gave my hair a second brushing. Then I locked up the house and left.

Ours is one of the older neighborhoods in New Orleans. In the new sections they make all the houses look alike. They just paint the shutters different colors so you can find your way home. But in our neighborhood, the houses are all different. Some are big old rambling places like Bridget's; others are neat little shingled squares like ours. The ancient trees lean out over the street, making a green archway for the cars. Their knotty roots buckle up the sidewalk, creating jumps for kids on bikes.

Our street, Lowerline, looks like one in a small town, but New Orleans is very cosmopolitan. People come here from all over the world. That's hard to believe, because on Lowerline everybody is pretty much the same. There are a few older people, like Mrs. Stebbins and the Pendletons, but it's mostly families.

Mrs. Stebbins's house, a small cottage, was white trimmed in yellow. A low white picket fence held back the tangle of flowers that leaned out toward the sidewalk.

When I reached the house, Mrs. Stebbins was bent over a flower bed with gardening tools in her gloved hands. A lock of white hair fell across her forehead. She pushed it away with the back of her hand.

"Mornin', Mrs. Stebbins."

She looked up at me through her frameless glasses. "Hello, Carrie. Good afternoon to you! Did you miss the morning today?"

"Yes, I did," I admitted, laughing. "I slept right through it."

"What luxury!" Mrs. Stebbins straightened up, putting her hand to her back. "I'm an early riser. Can't seem to kick the habit."

She seemed to be waiting for me to say more, and I realized I had never really stopped to talk with her in all the years she'd lived here. I vaguely remembered her moving in when my mom was in the hospital. There was an old man, too, but I hadn't paid much attention. Mom had died, and I didn't want to talk to anybody, especially an old person. When I was little I used to think old people were scary-looking.

"I, uh, Mrs. Stebbins, I'm looking for work today. I'm trying to earn some money."

"Oh?"

I nodded. I had been afraid to look closely at her before. She had a pretty face—tanned and filled with crinkly lines that turned up around her mouth and eyes. She wore a sundress the color of new leaves. It made her look cool even in the midday heat. "Yes, ma'am. You see, there's a special art workshop being offered in New York. My dad said if I could earn the money, maybe I could go."

"Mm. That sounds like a fine goal, Carrie."

"So I was wondering if I could do anything for you—anything at all."

"As a matter of fact, Carrie, I could use a helper. I was transplanting these bachelor buttons, and the weeds are overrunning the garden. It's all a little too much for my back these days. Do you like to garden, Carrie?"

"Yes, ma'am. I'd be happy to help."

I swung open the little gate and stepped into the yard. I had never gardened before and never particularly cared to. Mrs. Stebbins had to show me how to dig underneath the long-stemmed flowers and pull them gently, roots and all, from the earth. One by one, I dug them up, replanted them along the walkway to the house and watered them. Mrs. Stebbins stayed right by my side. I wondered at first if she was afraid I would botch it up.

"I understand how to do it now, Mrs. Stebbins," I told her, patting the soil around the third plant. "You can rest your back if you'd like."

"That's just what I should do." She sat down in the lawn chair, turning her tanned face toward the sun. In a few minutes, she was back at my side. "You're doing a fine job, Carrie," she said, "but you know, I just can't keep my hands out of these flowers. Let's work together, shall we?"

"Yes, ma'am. That's fine."

Mrs. Stebbins bent down and began digging out bachelor buttons. The lock of hair kept falling across her forehead, and she patiently pushed it back. Now and then, she put her hand to her back and straightened up for a moment. I knew her back must be aching. Mine was beginning to, but I kept changing positions to make it feel better. I guessed that wasn't so easy for Mrs. Stebbins.

She wasn't working on my account, I decided finally. She hadn't criticized anything I'd done, so I must have been doing okay. She must have loved working out there. I couldn't imagine why. It was hot and dirty. I decided that when I was as old as she was, I would kick off my shoes and relax. I would let people wait on me. But I'd better not think like that now, I reminded myself. I had plenty of work ahead if I was going to make that workshop.

"I wonder if these flowers suffer when we pull them out," I said. "They must think we're going to kill them."

Mrs. Stebbins laughed. "They say it helps to talk to them and to play them soft music. I suppose the people in the neighborhood would think I was a batty old lady if they caught me out here talking to the flowers."

I rested my arm on my knee and looked at her. "I wouldn't think so, Mrs. Stebbins. I would just think you liked your flowers a lot."

Mrs. Stebbins smiled. "I wish everyone was so understanding."

The sun burned down on us. I could feel little beads of sweat forming across my brow. Mrs. Stebbins disappeared into the house for a moment and came back with a big straw hat on her head and carrying one for me.

She sat down on the edge of her lawn chair and looked blankly at the garden.

"Mrs. Stebbins," I said, taking the hat out of her hand, "you all right?"

"Yes. Silly, but suddenly I can't remember where I left off."

"Over there, almost to the gate," I said, pointing to the spot.

"Yes, of course," she said softly and went back to work.

Finally the last bachelor button was transplanted. They stood in neat lines on either side of the walk, like tall soldiers with hats of pink, purple and blue. Mrs. Stebbins brushed her gloves against each other. "Now those weeds. Some of them are so pretty and strong, I'm tempted to let them be. I guess I would if they didn't choke the flowers."

She showed me which plants were weeds, and we set to work digging them out. I was surprised at how Mrs. Stebbins kept on. Between the heat and the work, I was ready to crawl off to the lawn chair. But I couldn't be the first to stop.

Mrs. Stebbins pulled out a sturdy bright-green plant and stopped to look at it. It had tiny yellow flowers bordered with white. They were the size of pinheads. "One day I'm going to plant a bed of the prettiest weeds," she said, "and invite *Better Homes and Gardens* to come see it!" She tossed the weed into the pile and pulled another. "Carrie, you're working mighty hard. This must be a very important workshop."

"Yes'm. It really is. Is this a weed?"

"No, that's a pea plant. You'll find a few hidden in here. It's an art workshop, you say?"

"Yes. But it's way up in New York State and it costs two hundred dollars for just two weeks."

I expected her to say that it was a long way or a lot of money, but she didn't say anything.

"My friend Bridget's uncle went to the same workshop years ago," I continued, "and he's a professional artist in New York City."

"And you would like to be a professional artist, too?"

"Yes'm. My dad says it's not steady work like nursing, which is what my sister wants to do, but I've always wanted to be an artist."

"Well, if you've wanted it that long, it must be important."

I glanced at her to see if she was making fun of me, but she wasn't. She was serious.

"I think I'd learn a lot at the workshop," I said eagerly. "I would also get to go to the galleries in New York. Besides, I've never been to New York."

"It sounds like a wonderful opportunity, Carrie. There's a lot to be learned just by traveling, too." Mrs. Stebbins stood up and fanned herself with her hat. "I would be pleased if you'd come work for me again soon, but let's stop for today. Come on inside. We'll have some lemonade and I'll get you your pay."

I had never been inside Mrs. Stebbins's house, but I thought it would be dark and musty-smelling and cluttered with pictures of smiling grandchildren. Instead, the house was cooled by air conditioning and as bright and fresh as outdoors. The sunshine glimmered in through the windows and lit upon the hanging plants. There were cut flowers in vases on nearly every table. I only saw one picture—that of a gray-haired man.

Mrs. Stebbins removed two glasses from the freezer and filled them with lemonade. "I keep one in here for myself, and one in case a friend should drop by. They get so nice and cold," she explained.

When I put my hand around the glass, my fingers melted their shape into the frost. Beneath the frost a pattern of yellow flowers was etched into the glass.

An orange-colored cat appeared in the doorway. It sprang up onto the counter and then leaped to the table to sniff my glass. It blinked its eyes solemnly and twitched its whiskers.

"Oh, Carrot," said Mrs. Stebbins, lifting the cat down. "Here, have some milk."

She sat down and smiled across at me. "Do you like cats, Carrie?"

Carrot passed his tongue across his mouth and

blinked up at me as if I were a fat sardine. My dog Toby had been dead only a couple of years, and I guess I was carrying on his tradition by hating cats. But you can't tell a cat lover you hate cats.

"Well, I'm more of a dog person," I explained, trying to be tactful. "We had a dog once, but he got hit by a car. My dad said no more pets for us."

"He doesn't care much for animals?"

I stirred my lemonade and watched the little bits of pulp swirl around and settle on the bottom again. "Oh, he does, but my mother died four years ago and then Toby died. I guess he didn't want to take another chance."

It had taken me a long time to learn to say—"my mother died." It took a long time for me to be able to say Toby died, too. A tiny brown ant had found a droplet of lemonade that had spilled from my glass. I crushed it with my pinky finger. Bugs should die, not people or pets.

I looked up, and Mrs. Stebbins was gazing at me. "You must have really wanted another dog to love and hold on to after losing both your mother and Toby."

I raised my eyebrows in surprise. It *would* have helped. After losing Toby, I had felt so empty. Times when Dad wasn't home and I would have gone to Mom, I got down on the floor and snuggled with Toby. Then there was nothing. But if there had been a new puppy ... "I think my mom would've said to get another dog, too. There are lots of great dogs that really need homes. You can't blame them because your own dog died."

"That's true," Mrs. Stebbins agreed. Carrot sprang up on her lap and she stroked him thoughtfully. He made a little rumbling noise inside. "But a lot of people feel like they couldn't love a second pet. Maybe your father feels that way."

"I guess so. I felt that way at first. Toby was the best, but I could still love another dog."

I glanced at my watch and gulped down my lemonade. "I better be going. It's almost our dinnertime."

"I hope you'll come back," said Mrs. Stebbins, handing me some folded bills. "I enjoyed having a helper. And I enjoyed your company even more."

"Thank you," I said, tucking the money into my pocket and blushing at her compliment. "I'll be back as soon as I can."

When I was just beyond her house, I pulled the money out and counted. Four dollars! I was off to a great start! Clenching the bills in my hand, I ran toward home.

CHAPTER

3

When I got home, Dad was in the kitchen making dinner with Sharon.

"Hi, honey," Dad said.

"Hi." I glanced at Sharon.

She smiled at me, her white, even teeth gleaming like an actress's in a toothpaste commercial. "Carrie, nice to see you again."

"Thanks." I averted my eyes slightly, avoiding the broad smile.

"I haven't seen you since summer vacation started. Are you enjoying yourself so far?"

"Oh, yeah. It's great," I said, without enthusiasm. I turned to Dad. "Is Phyllis sick?"

He looked at me in surprise. "No. Why do you ask?"

"I just wondered why she wasn't cooking dinner."

I saw Dad frown as I quickly left the kitchen. It galled me to come home and find Sharon puttering around. I always had to ask permission from Dad and Phyllis before I could invite a dinner guest, but nobody ever had to ask mine.

I went upstairs to my room, took the lid off the money jar on my desk and dropped in my earnings. I had twenty-three dollars there to start. Today's pay brought it up to twenty-seven. Two hundred dollars seemed like a long way off. And there was still the train fare.

"Carrie!" It was Dad.

I came out of my room and looked down the stair-well. "Sir?"

"Come down here, please."

I went downstairs and into the kitchen.

Dad stood over the cutting board and waved a peach toward Sharon. "Sharon offered to make dinner for us tonight. I think it would be nice if you'd set the table."

"Okay. Where's Phyllis?"

Dad whacked at the peach with a knife, found the pit and began digging it out. "Getting wheat germ and yogurt."

"Wheat germ and yogurt?"

Sharon smiled. "It's delicious in fruit salad, Carrie."

It sounded weird. I scooped up the flatware and went into the dining room. I carefully set the table with the forks and knives on the wrong side of the plates. Then I took away the vase of flowers Phyllis had brought in yesterday and put a fat ugly green candle I got three years ago in its place.

Phyllis breezed in moments later with a carton of yogurt and a jar of wheat germ, both in the family size. "They're much cheaper in these large sizes," she told Sharon.

Sharon nodded. "Especially if you're going to make them a regular part of your diet. They provide a lot of protein with very few calories."

I leaned against my chair, hoping they weren't going to talk about nutrition all night.

"I'm thinking of taking a slimnastics course this summer," said Phyllis, patting the roll around her waist. "You look so nice in slacks."

"Oh, thanks, Phyllis. I'm just lucky, I guess. I never put weight on."

When we all sat down, everyone waited for some-one else to start eating. Dad saw the candle and jumped up. "Candlelight dinner—what a good idea!" he said, putting a match to it.

I gave him a dry smile.

He reached for his fork as if it was always on the right-hand side and began eating. Sharon did the same. Phyllis looked at me coolly and speared some fruit salad. "Very tasty," she said.

"Phyllis makes great lasagna," I said.

"We're big on Italian food," Dad added.

"Great!" said Sharon. "I know a little Italian res-taurant downtown that has super antipasto."

"Guido's?" Phyllis asked.

"Yes."

"Oh, I love it! Al and I go there. Maybe we could all go sometime."

I gave Phyllis a dirty look. She just smeared butter on a muffin and bit off half. I pictured her eating her way through a muffin as big as a house. She'd get bigger and bigger, like a balloon. Then I imagined her floating through the air like the Goodyear blimp.

I must have been smiling because Sharon looked at me as if she wondered what the joke was.

Dad turned eagerly to Sharon. "Phyllis is starting nursing school this fall."

Phyllis smiled, waiting to hear for the umpteenth time what a wonderful profession nursing was—so necessary and noble. And so practical.

"And I'm going to an art workshop this August," I said.

Sharon shifted her water-blue eyes to me. "That sounds interesting."

Dad waved his hand. "Oh, it's something her friend Bridget got her into—I doubt she'll go."

"It's kind of expensive," I explained. "So I have to earn the money, including the fare to New York." That's good, I thought. Let her know Dad isn't rich.

"Money's only one thing, Carrie," Dad said. "There are other factors, as I mentioned."

"Like what?"

"You're a little young to go traipsing off to New York," he said.

"Bridget's uncle Greg left home when he was only sixteen," I countered. "That's only four years older than me. He got a job and later got a scholarship to an art school and now he's a successful artist. He told Bridget that being responsible for yourself is one of the best ways to learn. I think it'd be better to travel some before I'm out on my own, though, don't you?"

Dad jabbed his fork into an orange section and dunked it into the yogurt. "You've got quite a few years before you need to think about that," he said. "Well beyond sixteen, I'd say."

I knew Dad didn't like getting into this discussion in front of Sharon, but I didn't care.

"I bet a lot of people would pay for the kind of tour her uncle's going to give us." I was wound up now. "And who knows, I might meet some important people—maybe somebody who will want to pay for my education. That happens sometimes."

"Carrie, we can put you through school."

"Yeah, but it'd be nice to get it free, wouldn't it? I've heard it's very expensive, and besides, lots of artists have patrons."

"I hardly think—"

"It does happen, Dad. Bridget told me about this sculptor—"

Dad shook his head. "Not now, Carolyn. Just remember, I've made no promises." He turned in his seat and glanced at Phyllis. "Did I tell you that Sharon runs the Good Sports Shop in town? She was transferred from a much smaller store in Slidell."

Phyllis murmured a polite note of interest.

I pushed the fruit salad around on my plate. "My mother designed children's clothing," I told Sharon. "She was the best designer at the Small Wonders Company. Everyone said she was very creative. I guess I get my talent from her."

A little cloud passed over Dad's eyes and vanished.

"Your mother must have been very special," said Sharon.

"Oh, she was," I assured her. "Once you've had a mother like her, you don't need anyone else. You know what I mean?"

There was a moment of silence. Dad flushed, Phyllis glowered and Sharon sat motionless, her eyes still and thoughtful. I took a forkful of fruit salad and smiled pleasantly.

"It must be gratifying to share an interest with your mother," Sharon said at last.

"Carrie does some very clever cartoons," Dad conceded.

The tension was broken. Phyllis sighed audibly, and Dad changed the subject quickly. "Sharon's quite an athlete," he said.

"Oh, Jack!" she protested. "I just jog and swim for fun."

"And water-ski and play tennis. In fact," he said, turning to Phyllis and me, "I'm going to start jogging with her soon."

"Exercise is good for the heart," pronounced Phyllis, reaching for her third muffin.

A picture of Phyllis stuffed into a track outfit with a candy bar in each hand flashed through my mind. I popped a slice of apple into my mouth to keep from laughing.

"While we're tooting horns," said Sharon, "I hope you girls realize what an accomplished accountant your father is. The books were a mess when I took over the store and Good Sports called on your father's firm. Your dad not only did an expert audit, but he gave me a clear picture of what was selling in the area."

"You had pretty much figured out what merchandise would move," said Dad.

"Still, it helps to have the figures to confirm it," Sharon replied. "There are general trends, but an area often has special interests. And a mistake in ordering can be very costly."

"That was how you met, wasn't it?" asked Phyllis.

"Yes. Your dad spent a good two weeks untangling things—although I must say I wondered if he wasn't stretching it a little toward the end!"

"Oh, all in the line of work!" Dad protested.

"You always bring in lunch for your clients?"

"Absolutely," said Dad, laughing.

Dinner was an ordeal. Everybody went on to talk

about Sharon's store. After my moment of triumph, I became a spectator. Although everyone included me in their glances around the table and their general comments, they seemed satisfied that I was quiet.

I did the dishes as quickly as I could and retreated to my bedroom, leaving Dad and Sharon chattering in the living room and Phyllis reading some novel about nurses that she had bought at the supermarket.

I looked at the picture of my mother on the dresser. Her face smiled out at me. She had always been a port of refuge. I remembered the time in first grade I had had an argument with a friend. She had been so angry that she had invited everybody in the class to her birthday party except me. I was crushed. But Mom had taken me out to lunch and a movie on the day of the party. It had been my first lunch in a real restaurant. It hadn't taken away the hurt, but it had made me feel a lot better.

I think I was closer to Mom than Phyllis had been. Phyllis had learned how to sew from Mom, which I never had, but all she did was fix hems and seams and follow simple patterns for skirts and shifts. She couldn't do anything on her own. Mom and I would spend a whole afternoon designing clothes for my paper dolls. She once said my designs gave her some ideas she was able to use. Mom and Phyllis had been mother and daughter, but Mom and I had been something more.

I flopped down on my bed and pulled out my sketch pad and pencils from underneath. I flipped to a blank page and began drawing a cartoon of Sharon. I drew her wearing a bathing suit, with muscles bulging, crossed eyes and feathers instead of hair. Beneath it I wrote: "Featherhead."

Then Dad called, "Carrie, Sharon's leaving!"

I didn't go out. I just yelled, " 'Bye!" Dad probably didn't like that, but I didn't care. I watched out the window as she left. Dad walked out to her yellow hatchback and kissed her. Then she climbed in and rode away.

When Dad came in to say good night, he sat down on the side of my bed and looked at me very seriously. "Sometimes new things are hard to accept," he said. "Carrie, Sharon is a wonderful woman, and she's very special to me. I hope you will give her a chance."

"I will, Dad," I said.

"At a time like this it's natural to think of your mother," he went on, "to think of how much you love and miss her, to feel that no one could take her place." He glanced over at Mom's picture. I wondered if he felt that he was betraying her.

"But no one is trying to replace her. No one can take her away from you. That doesn't mean we have to close ourselves off from other people."

He paused, and I just looked at him. I suppose he wanted me to say that I didn't really mind his going out with Sharon. If he was looking to me for permission, he wasn't going to get it.

"Do you understand what I'm saying?"

"Yes." I pulled the sheet up to my chin and yawned.

"Well," he said awkwardly, "guess I'd better let you get to sleep." He patted me on the head and left.

Outside my door, I could hear Phyllis on the phone with Al. They'd been going together for four years and they still talked for hours on the telephone.

In my darkened room, the loneliness settled around me like a cloak. I thought of Mrs. Stebbins's house, the flowers popping open in the sunshine. Somewhere in the distance, a riverboat sounded its horn, and I drifted off to sleep.

CHAPTER
4

One evening a week later, I walked into Dad's room to find a dozen or so new thick white socks with colored stripes around the top lying on his bed. Dad had always worn thin black socks.

"What're those for?" I asked him.

"Jogging." He opened up a shoe box and pulled out a pair of brilliant blue nylon shoes with yellow orange stripes. "I got some running shoes, too. Got them wholesale at Sharon's store."

"What's wrong with your old ones?"

He looked at his black canvas sneakers and laughed. "They're no good for running. See, look at the cushioning on these shoes. Look at the tread on the sole. We'll have to get you fitted for a pair soon."

"No thanks," I told him. "When I have to wear shoes, my sandals will do just fine."

"Sure, but you can't run in sandals."

"Who's running?"

Dad didn't answer but set the new shoes in his closet and put the socks in his drawer. I noticed he was still letting his hair grow. He could comb it back on the sides now, and in the back it crept to the top of his collar. Soon he and Sharon would have matching hairstyles.

Suddenly I thought about the workshop and knew I had to go. Not just for what I'd learn but to get away. I wondered if Dad would miss me while I was gone. Maybe he'd wish I was home and we were watching the Saturday night movie together like in the old days. Then he'd know how I felt.

That week I went to Mrs. Stebbins's every day. Dad told me not to make a pest of myself. He thought I might be making her feel that she ought to give me something to do. But Mrs. Stebbins seemed to be waiting for me to come each day. Either she'd be out puttering in the garden or she was sitting in her lawn chair, saying she wanted to get to work and just needed a nudge.

One morning I noticed that several of the bachelor buttons I'd transplanted along the walkway were shriveling up. I showed them to Mrs. Stebbins, thinking she'd be upset.

"Yes, I noticed those," she said. Then, seeing my face, she gave me a little hug. "Don't feel bad. We were bound to lose a few in the transplanting. See those over by the fence? They're still a little crowded. We'll get our replacements there."

I picked up my trowel and we went to work. "Mrs. Stebbins," I said, "your place is so peaceful."

"Why, thank you, Carrie," she said. "I've felt that way about it, too."

Encouraged, I went on. "It seems like you're always happy. Doesn't anything get you down?"

She smiled. "Oh, now and then. But I've found that most things usually don't deserve the fuss and worry people give them. What about you, Carrie? Are things getting you down?"

I plunged my trowel into the earth and began jiggling a flower out of its resting place. "No, not really," I said. "Let's put the pink buttons along the walk. We don't have too many pinks there."

"That would brighten it up."

The weather stayed hot and muggy. I was dripping with sweat at the end of each day and my dark skin was turning deep brown. After a while I actually liked the weeding. I was clearing a place to give those beautiful flowers a chance. Every day the garden grew prettier. Mrs. Stebbins had a few vegetable plants scattered among the flowers. She was planning to dig out a whole bed for vegetables next year and she said I could help her with the planting. I wondered whether a seed I put in the ground would grow.

On Sunday, Bridget came over early. In my room she set up the spattered easel she'd had since she was nine and laid out her oil paints and brush. She had bought a big canvas on sale in the French Quarter. She propped it up on the easel and began to paint. Her painting was of eyes—no faces, just eyes. They were all different sizes and in brilliant shades of pink, chartreuse and yellow. She said she hadn't planned it, but that she just felt moved to do an interpretive study of the human eye. I thought it was weird, but I didn't say so.

I had my trusty sketch pad and pencils and was drawing a cartoon of Bridget painting. It wasn't a mean cartoon like the one I'd done of Sharon. I just took the most important things about Bridget and exaggerated them. I made her big, floppy hat twice as big. I had her long, brown hair, which she parts in the middle, cover all of her face but a narrow line. Today she was wearing some new black false eyelashes; I drew them standing out like brushes. The more I looked at her, the more she looked like a struggling artist, so I drew her eyes deep and dark.

"So, Carrie," she drawled, "how's life in the love nest?"

"Very funny. It stinks. Turn your face back a little toward me."

"Is the wicked witch in jogging shoes still stirring up trouble?"

"Is she ever! She and Dad have been bugging me to think of things we could all do together—"

"They want you to dig your own grave."

"Right. Sharon is plowing right in. Phyllis likes her, and it looks serious with Dad."

Bridget stopped in the middle of the eye she was

working on. "Maybe you're not coming on strong enough. If it seems like too much of a hassle, she'll back off. Or your dad will."

"Believe me, I haven't been nice. Sometimes I feel guilty about being such a creep, but I can't just sit back and take it."

Bridget turned back to her canvas. "You've got to let them know how you feel."

"I wish it made more of a difference. Don't those eyelashes make your lids tired?"

"It's worth the agony."

I was just shading in the hair when Dad rapped once on the door and came in, holding a newspaper clipping. His eyes widened a little, and he stared at Bridget's painting. He scratched his head. "It's bright," he said. Then he looked at mine. A faint smile crossed his lips. I was glad I wasn't drawing Sharon or Phyllis.

"Why aren't you girls outside?" he asked. "It's a beautiful day."

Bridget held her brush in the air and flapped her new eyelashes. "Mr. Moyer, when you are thirteen you have other things on your mind."

"Or twelve," I added.

"I see." Dad looked at the newspaper clippng in his hand. "Oh, this is what I wanted to tell you about. It says here there's a two-week art class given by the Recreation Department. It starts tomorrow at ten A.M."

"Mr. Moyer, those things are for little kids," Bridget explained.

"It says here nine through thirteen."

"Oh, Dad," I said, "that's nothing compared to the workshop."

"My uncle—" Bridget began.

A vein twitched in Dad's forehead and his face stiffened. "I've heard enough about your uncle, Bridget. One thing you girls don't seem to realize is that you don't know it all and even this Mr."— he glanced at the clipping—"Stewart from the Recreation Department might be able to teach you something!" He marched out of the room and slammed the door.

I set down my pencil and took a deep breath. There was a knot in my stomach. Bridget was standing there with her hand on her hip and an amazed expression on her face. "What brought that on?" she asked finally.

I shrugged. "I dunno."

"I never told him about my uncle before—did I?"

"No. But I've been telling him."

"He doesn't think that class would be as good as the workshop, does he?"

"No, probably not. He's just hoping I'll forget about it. He doesn't think I can raise the money anyway."

For a moment, neither of us spoke. I sat down on the edge of my bed.

"Hey, Carrie, I've got an idea. We could take our easels to the French Quarter and paint at Jackson

Square. We'll put out a collection hat and a sign, 'Help send art students to school.' "

I had to smile at the image of people dropping spare change into one of Bridget's hats while we painted. Phyllis had been called in to work today. That'd be about the time she'd decide to walk through the square on her lunch hour. "Nah, I don't think so. I think I'll just go over to Mrs. Stebbins's. She's had a lot of work for me." I started putting my pencils away.

"Well, wait a little bit. My painting's still wet."

"I can't, Bridget. I've got to get out of here." I knew my stomach would stay knotted until I left. "You can leave your painting here to dry," I added.

"Okay." Bridget sighed, packing up her paints and brushes. "I still say you'd make more at the square."

I could hear Dad downstairs vacuuming the rugs—something he liked to do when he was mad. I scrawled a note saying that I would be at Mrs. Stebbins's and left it on the refrigerator.

The sidewalk burned my bare feet and I had to hop from one grassy patch to the next, watching out for the honey bees that hovered over the dandelions.

Mrs. Stebbins had her back to me and I leaned on the fence for a moment to watch her. She wore a pale flowered sundress and a large straw hat. In her hand was a metal watering can. She reminded me of a print of a little girl with a watering can I'd seen at the Art

Center. Mrs. Stebbins was the girl all grown up. I wished I could feel comfortable wearing sundresses instead of cutoffs all the time.

Then Mrs. Stebbins raised her head and turned toward me. "Hello, Carrie."

"Hi."

"Looking for a job?"

"I guess . . . no, not really. I just wanted to get out of the house."

"You look kind of down in the mouth today," she observed.

"Yes'm. My dad yelled at my best friend, Bridget. I think he's getting to hate her. He wants me to forget about the art workshop and go to an art class being offered by the Recreation Department."

"That does sound bad." Mrs. Stebbins pushed the lock of hair off her forehead. "Come on inside. Let's have some lemonade."

I followed her into the house, feeling a little uneasy.

Mrs. Stebbins laid her straw hat and gloves on a little table in the foyer and headed for the kitchen. On the kitchen table lay a bag of African violet food, some small plastic pots and a carton of Kitty Treats. She pushed these to one end and then turned to get our drinks.

I stood watching her, running my fingers over the wicker backing of the kitchen chair. If I was to do a caricature of her, I decided, it would all be slight, thin strokes. Ink would be the thing to use.

The coolness of the house settled around me and I began to relax. Mrs. Stebbins was emptying ice from the tray when we heard a knock at the door.

"I'll get it."

I bounded over to the front door and swung it open to find Mrs. Pendleton, the lady from across the street, standing there with a box in her hand.

"Carolyn!" she said, looking surprised. "Is Mrs. Stebbins here?"

"Yes, she—"

"Goodness, I hope I'm not interrupting." She breezed past me toward the kitchen. "Miss Grace? Hello!"

"Hello, Harriet. Come in," Mrs. Stebbins answered.

I followed Mrs. Pendleton into the kitchen. Mrs. Stebbins had left the empty glasses on the counter and seated herself at the table.

"Have I come at a bad time? You have guests?" She glanced around as if expecting to see someone more important than me standing in the corner.

"Carrie and I were having a visit."

Mrs. Pendleton smiled. "Oh. How nice. Do pardon me, Carolyn dear. I won't be a minute. Miss Grace, I've brought those envelopes."

"Envelopes?" The sunlight, streaming in the window, caught Mrs. Stebbins's glasses and they glinted briefly. Looking over Mrs. Pendleton's broad shoulder, I was struck by how delicate and tiny Mrs. Stebbins looked.

"Yes, for the Ladies of Good Cheer Club," said Mrs. Pendleton. She set the box down in front of Mrs. Stebbins. "You agreed to address them. Have you forgotten?"

Mrs. Stebbins picked up the list of names on top of the stack of envelopes and gazed at it. She had the look of someone searching in a pool of water for something lost on the bottom.

"Mary Cable called you, dear. Last week. I hope you can still help us with it. You remember Mary calling, don't you?"

Mrs. Stebbins picked up the box of envelopes and carried them into the living room. "It slipped my mind, I suppose, Harriet. But, of course, if I said I'd do them, I will."

"Oh dear. Perhaps it's an inconvenience now. Other things must have come up. And we do need them next week—"

"No, it's perfectly all right, Harriet." Mrs. Stebbins walked her to the door.

"The Ladies of Good Cheer are in your debt, of course," Mrs. Pendleton continued.

"The ladies are entirely welcome," said Mrs. Stebbins.

She closed the door firmly behind Mrs. Pendleton and turned to me. "Now, where were we?"

"The lemonade," I said. "I'll pour."

This time the glasses from the freezer had a daisy print on them. I filled them with lemonade and ice, and we sat down. Mrs. Stebbins was as relaxed with me, I thought, as if I were another white-haired lady she'd known since she was three.

I scratched the back of my leg with a bare toe. "You must have friends dropping by all the time," I said.

She smiled. "Not really. I've made some very nice friends since I've been in New Orleans, but, of course, people are involved with their own lives, and I've become more solitary than I was a few years back."

"How about your kids? They must come a lot, don't they?"

"No, unfortunately Edward and I never had any children."

"Oh. You must get kind of lonely."

"From time to time, but it passes. Most things do. I keep busy and I try to make new friends—like you! Which reminds me—'Mrs. Stebbins' sounds so formal. Couldn't we make it Grace? That sounds so much more friendly."

"Okay, Grace," I said. It felt strange to call a woman with white hair by her first name. But it was nice, too. I hoped that if I ever got to be her age, I'd be as content. More likely, I'd still be grouching around.

"What sort of class does your father want you to go to, Carrie?" Grace asked.

"Oh, it's an art class, but not serious."

"Not like the workshop."

"No. It's probably just for little kids."

"You are very determined to become an artist, aren't you?"

I nodded.

"Well, I think you'll succeed, Carrie. I expect you won't let any opportunity pass you by."

Just then there was a piercing screech outside. Grace hurried to the door. She sighed. "It's Carrot. He's up in that tree again. It just doesn't look like we're going to have a quiet chat today, Carrie."

We went outside and saw Carrot sitting high in the oak tree. He blinked mournfully down at us.

"Won't he come down?" I asked.

Grace shook her head. "He always climbs that tree, but he's scared to death to come down."

"But that's not natural," I said. "Cats are great climbers."

"Not this one," said Grace. "This one's afraid and we'll just have to help him along until he gets over it. There's a ladder around the side of the house. Would you rescue him, Carrie? I usually do it, but I shouldn't be up on ladders."

"Sure."

Carrot didn't claw me as I had expected. He just

snuggled up against my chest and purred. He was kind of dumb, but all the same, he was nice. I wondered if my old dog, Toby, would have made an exception for him.

After Carrot was safely down, I got an old basket and some rope from our attic. I hung the rope over the branch Carrot had been on and tied one end to the basket so that Grace could rescue him without a ladder. Then we went in and finished our lemonade.

"The flowers are in good shape now," said Grace, "but I have some other work that needs doing—if you're still in business."

"Yes, ma'am—Grace," I said. "I'm still in business."

"Good! Tomorrow morning, then?"

"Okay."

"We talked a little about the art class. Was something else getting you down?"

"No, not really." I sipped the last of my lemonade and looked out toward the garden. "I didn't really want to talk about anything. I was just mad about the workshop."

"Thinking your dad wanted you to go to the class instead?"

"Yeah." A thought was forming. Why not go to both? I still wasn't excited about it, or any less excited about the workshop, but maybe it was, as Grace suggested, an opportunity. There must be something there for me. And it would make Dad happy. "Could we work in the afternoon tomorrow?" I asked. "I think I'll try that recreation class—it can't hurt."

Grace pushed back the lock of hair and smiled. "Fine."

CHAPTER
5

I was the oldest one attending the art class at the center near us. I don't think the other kids were interested in art. They were just looking for something to do in the summer. Or maybe their mothers sent them to get them out of the house.

We sat on benches by a long table. There was a lengthy wait while the little kids sat swinging their legs and poking each other in the ribs. Mr. Stewart, perched on a table in front, tugged his moustache and watched the bedlam. I sat at the far end of the table, my chin in my hand, wondering if Dad had ever been to one of these things.

Finally, Mr. Stewart rose and, running his fingers through the thick hair that hung down his neck, welcomed us. He was an art teacher from Benjamin Franklin Senior High, he told us, and "really pleased to be working with kids who have a fresh outlook on things."

On the first day we were to make tissue-paper flow-

ers. I hate fake flowers. I like drawing, period. I was glad
Bridget wasn't there.

I started to make a flower. Some of the little kids
were covering their faces with tissue paper and looking
toward the sunlight that streamed in through the windows of the bald, square room. Others started folding
their tissue to make their flowers, forgot how to do it
and raised their hands for help. Mr. Stewart hovered
over everyone, praising and making suggestions. When
kids talked to him, he opened his eyes real wide, as if
they were telling him the most amazing thing.

Then I saw the supply closet. It was filled with all
sorts of things I didn't have at home—charcoal, India
ink and good drawing paper. I took out some charcoal
and paper and settled in the corner to draw.

Mr. Stewart saw me and came over. "Don't you
want to make flowers to take home?"

"Not really. I just want to draw."

He looked baffled. Then he said, "Okay."

At the end of the class he came up behind me and
looked over my shoulder. He wouldn't have seen my
picture otherwise. It was a cartoon of him with great big
wings and a beak, hovering over the kids. He had
round, owl eyes.

A grin crept over his face. He laughed. "It's good.
It really is!"

I grinned back.

"This owl here—this Mr. Stewart," he went on,

"the contours are great. He's tangible. I could reach out and touch this wing."

He really does like it, I thought, even though I'm making fun of him.

"I have a suggestion. If you give Mr. Stewart a little more contrast—make the blacks blacker—it'll bring him out and give a feeling of depth."

I shaded in the wing and darkened the outline, and sure enough, the owl-man seemed closer, as if he'd fly right off the page.

I took the charcoal back to the closet and left for Grace's. She had been right. This was an opportunity to learn more.

Grace had a sandwich and lemonade ready when I arrived.

"Carrie, there's a job I've been waiting to get done for a long time, but I've needed a helper. I want to make an indoor greenhouse."

"How can you do that?"

"With lights, mainly. There'll be some window space. I'll convert the china cabinet into an enclosed greenhouse for the plants that like high humidity."

"Where will the greenhouse be?"

"In the den. That's our job today. We've got to pack it up. It's full of my husband's things—his old lawbooks, notes, awards and what not. It's been like a museum since he died and I can't see the point of that."

"That's what my dad did."

"What?"

"Packed up all my mom's stuff after she died—her clothing, her sketchboard, her mannequin. Everything that was hers." I felt an edge coming into my voice. After Mom died, Phyllis and I went to stay with our grandparents in Shreveport for two weeks. I still remember the ache I felt when I walked into the house and noticed that her stuff was gone.

"Were you angry?"

"Yes." I wasn't sure I wanted to talk about it. Grace was planning to do the same thing. I didn't want to get mad at her, but I was afraid I might if we talked more about it. I thought of making some excuse to leave, but instead I sat there, fingering a leftover crust of bread.

"You wanted everything left as it was," she said.

"Yes. To make me feel as if she was still there. Sometimes I still go to the attic to look through Mom's old scrapbooks and to touch her stuff. If I was boss at our house," I said heatedly, "I wouldn't have moved a thing."

"It would have been a memorial."

"Yes. Only you said 'museum' before. People don't care about museums. They care about memorials!" I felt my face flush. I should have left earlier.

"You're right about that," she said softly. "That's why I want to pack up the den. It is a museum now, unused. But I want to make it a memorial."

"But you said a greenhouse."

She smiled. "Yes. My husband loved to see the garden and to have houseplants. I'd always kept a few and everyone exclaimed over them. I seemed to have special luck with plants and had them blooming when no one else did."

She stacked the empty plates together and pushed them aside. "Edward was always after me to do something special for myself. Once he even said, 'Grace, you've such a knack with plants, you ought to open up a nursery.' Well, I sloughed it off with excuses. It would be a lot of work, I had too many other things to do and so on. Now, finally, I'm going to take his advice and do something special for myself. So, you see, it will be in memory of my husband. A memorial."

For a moment neither of us spoke. I felt confused. Grace was doing something for herself, but it was for her husband, too. It seemed strange. I could tell she loved him and wasn't trying to forget him.

"Edward taught me to find out what I wanted in life and go after it. What did your mother teach you?"

"Well, Mom was a designer. She was very good," I answered thoughtfully. "I guess she tried to teach me to look at things in new ways."

"Wonderful. Perhaps your unique vision will lead you to do something that will be a memorial for her."

"But what?"

"Ah. You'll have to think on that. You'll hit on it

one day, and it will feel just right." She put our dishes in the sink and laid a hand on my shoulder. "Come along now and help me with my memorial."

Grace had been getting ready for that afternoon. The den was cluttered with boxes and the shelves were nearly empty. She was going to finish the packing while I carried the boxes to the attic. But when I tried to pick up the first box, I couldn't. "Oh dear," said Grace. "I've made these too heavy."

"What's in here?"

"Lawbooks, mainly. They're enormous things."

We opened it up and began pulling some of the books out. "My husband used to pore over these books when he was working on a case," Grace commented, laying a volume on the desk. "I enjoy reading, but I could never spend the hours he did with one of these." She laughed softly. "I used to say, 'Edward, come and walk with me before the darkness falls,' and he'd say, 'In a minute. I'm hunting an answer here.' Like as not, the night would come and he'd still be hunting. He did enjoy his work so. Having so much time on my hands, I had trouble understanding that sometimes. I guess that's why he encouraged me to find my own labor of love."

I tested the weight of the half-filled box and found that I could carry it. "I can put more books in it when I'm in the attic so you don't run out of boxes," I suggested.

"That's a good idea."

Instead of hoisting the box up and away, I looked at her. I'd never thought about her having another life before she came here. I wondered what she had been like when she was young. "Grace, what did you do when your husband was a lawyer? Were you a teacher or something?"

"No, I was a lady of leisure, as they say. We lived in Atlanta then. Edward was quite successful. I was involved in charity work—fund-raising, that sort of thing."

"Didn't you ever wish you had a job?" I asked.

Grace drew a handkerchief from her pocket and began polishing her glasses. "In those days, women didn't go out and do things unless they had to. I didn't give it much thought at the time, I guess. But, looking back, I would have liked that nursery Edward suggested—I'd have raised all sorts of lovely plants."

"Why didn't you do it, then?"

"I was busy. Edward used to ask me, 'Grace, do you really want to organize this dance for the children's home? Do you really want to be treasurer of that city park fund?' And I'd tell him, 'Certainly. It's a worthy cause.'" She tucked the handkerchief back into her pocket and replaced her glasses. Then she pulled a penknife across the tape sealing another box. "I just didn't realize I wanted something for myself." She smiled and added sheepishly, "Sometimes I still slip back to old ways and take on jobs I don't truly want to do."

"Like Mrs. Pendleton and the envelopes."

"Yes. Like that."

"You must be mad, losing all those years when you could've had your nursery."

"No, not mad. They were good years. The charity work was important, but there were a lot of vacant hours—time wiled away at tea parties and club meetings. So much time lost to trivia."

"Are you going to start a nursery now?"

Grace laughed. "It's a little late for that. I'll be happy with the greenhouse, though. You know, you're fortunate, Carrie—a person with her eyes toward the goal, Edward would have said. I didn't realize how much I'd have liked a nursery until I was in my seventies. Here you are, twelve years old and on your way to becoming an artist."

Grace would've liked Mom, I thought. Mom went after what she wanted. Dad must have been proud of her for that, too. I remember, when Mom called Dad "the breadwinner," he called her "the butter winner." Mom used to say, "Now it's up to you girls to win the cheese." I had just laughed when she said it, not understanding what she meant. Now I thought she meant that she expected us to go out and achieve too, to use our talents.

"Carrie, I'd love to see some of your artwork," Grace was saying. "Won't you bring me some soon?"

"Oh, well, they're only sketches."

"I like sketches."

"Okay."

I wrapped my arms around the box and carted it off to the attic. The attic was a barren, sloping room. It didn't look like anyone had ever been up there. Ours was so full of junk it was hard to find anything. I set the box down against one wall and trotted back to the den for a second.

As I was carrying the second box through the living room, my eyes fell on Mr. Stebbins's picture. I stopped, setting the box on the floor. I couldn't get over the feeling that Grace and I were not respecting him. When Mom died, I felt I owed her something—the pain of missing her, the treatment of her belongings as special for the memories they held. It was a way of holding her place in life open.

I wandered back to the den. "Was it terrible for you when your husband died?"

"It was hard. We'd had a long, wonderful life together. I hadn't really considered being without him."

"When my mom died, I couldn't believe it. Then I got mad. I practically hated everybody who had a mother. Now I feel sad about it. Sometimes I wish I was a little kid again, before she got cancer."

Grace's eyes were sympathetic. "I remember feeling I'd like to sit right down in my easy chair and never move again. If Edward couldn't live, neither would I. But then I realized that people who love us don't want us to stop living when they do. Edward would have been appalled at the thought of my wilting away simply because I was alone."

"But everything changes when somebody important dies," I said.

"Yes, death does change things," Grace agreed, "but we change as we grow, too. We keep our loved ones in our hearts; that's enough."

I nodded and went back to work. Grace's words had filled me up. Dad and Phyllis were often afraid to talk to me about feelings, but Grace didn't back away from anything I said.

It took us the whole afternoon to get the boxes up to the attic. Finally, the only thing left to do was move the furniture. When we pushed the desk away from the wall, we discovered an old picture that had fallen. It was their wedding picture. I wondered whether Grace would burst into tears.

Instead, she smiled. Then she put a nail in the wall by the window and hung up the picture. "I'd wondered what had become of this picture. It will be a wonderful way to dedicate the greenhouse."

I smiled. Mom and Dad's wedding picture had disappeared about a year ago. "Anything else you want done here?" I asked.

"No, that's it for now. I'm worn out. The doctor says I should slow down, but I'm afraid I'm not a very good patient." She sat down on the desk chair. "And I think I've run you into your dinnertime besides."

I glanced at my watch. "I guess I should get on home."

Grace pressed some money into my hand. "I hope today hasn't upset you, Carrie."

"Well, it did at first," I confessed. "But now I'm glad I helped. Can I help you set up the greenhouse?"

"Of course you can. It's really our project now."

At home, some dopey love movie was on TV. Al was slouched on the sofa with his arm around Phyllis. The sofa had worked its way toward the center of the room again and the coffee table had ceased to be a window seat. I could barely see Al's head over the sofa, but those big number-thirteen sneakers propped up on the coffee table were unmistakable. Dad once told me Al's feet had grown faster than the rest of him, but that things would eventually even up. Al's nineteen. I think he's running out of time.

"Hi," I said.

Phyllis mumbled, "Wait a minute—the TV . . ."

Al just grunted. He'd been coming around for so many years that he acted like he lived here. He didn't even give me a decent hello. I was beginning to wonder who was the outsider.

I was hungry, so I walked into the kitchen. There was nothing in the oven. "What's for dinner?" I called.

Suddenly Dad and Sharon burst in the door. They were both wearing jogging shorts and tank tops. Dad looked strange. His shirt was wringing wet and he was panting.

"Boy, do I feel great!" he exclaimed. "Let's all go jogging tomorrow!"

I groaned.

Dad leaned on the table with one hand and put the other on his side. "Whew!"

"You okay, Dad?"

"Just got a cramp." He was still gasping for breath.

"You need to walk around until you catch your breath," said Sharon. "It's not good to stop until you do."

Dad began walking in circles around the kitchen.

"Where do you jog to?" I asked.

"Just around a couple of blocks to start," said Sharon. She ran her fingers through the thatch of hair at her neck.

"What's the point of running, if you're not going anywhere?"

"Why, for the fun of it," said Dad, still panting.

"Oh." He looked like a breathless man in salty, soggy shorts, not like a man in love with jogging.

"You'll have to forgive him," Sharon told me with a comradely air. "New converts are always overzealous. Jogging is not for everyone."

I looked at her blandly, then turned back to my father. "I'm hungry."

"Good. As soon as we shower and change, we'll all go out to dinner."

I groaned again. "I'm tired. I've been working hard. Couldn't I just stay home?"

"You'll feel better when we get there, Carrie. Besides, this is special. I want everyone to go."

Special. The word gave me a sudden chill. What could be special about this dinner? I had a feeling it had to do with more than a nice restaurant or the fact that we would all be there. I tried to find the answer in his face, but he turned and, taking Sharon's hand, showed her to the towels.

I went to my room and changed. The shower was still running. I rested on my bed. Finally Dad called me, and I met them in front off the house.

We all piled into our car, me in the back with Phyllis and Al. As big as Phyllis and Al were, they managed to squeeze together, leaving about a foot of space between them and me. Sharon rested her arm on the back of her seat and turned to face me.

"You know, Carrie, my roommate in college— Peggy Anderson—majored in art."

"Mm," I mumbled. I looked at the passing trees, pretending to be engrossed with the scenery.

Sharon wouldn't take the hint. "She dabbled around in this and that and finally settled on making pottery. Did you ever try it?"

"We made clay ashtrays in kindergarten."

Sharon laughed, her blond lashes veiling her eyes momentarily. "She's gotten a bit more sophisticated than that. Has her own wheel. Maybe you'd like to visit her sometime. She lives just over in Baton Rouge."

"Does she make her living selling pottery?"

"No. She teaches art in an elementary school."

I made a face. "People only teach when they're not good enough—especially in elementary schools."

Sharon's face betrayed the sting, but she wrinkled her brow and tried again. "That may be true sometimes, but Peggy took a double major—education and art. She loved them both. I think you'd enjoy meeting her."

I looked away. "No, thanks," I said. "I'm not interested in pottery. Besides, I'll be meeting plenty of real artists at the workshop."

Dad shifted the car down and it jerked us all forward. The engine groaned until he put it back into high gear. I could feel Sharon's eyes on me for a moment and, out of the corner of my eye, saw her lay a quieting hand on Dad's arm.

Sharon, Dad, Phyllis and Al began talking about college. Phyllis talked with her so easily. How could she? How could she like her so much, she who was so much older than I when Mom died? I felt a sudden sadness. I could not have felt more alone had I been riding with four strangers.

We pulled up at the Tea House, a nice Chinese restaurant. We went there occasionally. The owner, who Dad had done some accounting for, greeted us at the door and bowed slightly.

"Good evening, Mr. Moyer," he said, smiling. "We have a special table prepared for you and your party."

As he led us to our place, Al tripped over a statue

and nearly broke it. We all pretended not to notice.

The table was tucked away in a private corner. It had paper lanterns hanging all around it. Every place had a stiff cloth napkin, a little china teacup and a pair of chopsticks. A waiter brought us a pot of tea right away and silverware for everyone.

We all took seats. I found myself sitting across from Sharon and considered moving to the empty chair next to me, but I knew I would only draw daggers. Dad and Phyllis seemed intent on having a good time. I studied the birds of Louisiana that were pictured on the sugar packets in the center of the table.

When the menu came, I didn't look at it. I always order chicken chow mein. Dad told the waiter he wanted moo goo gai pan.

"But, Dad, you always get egg foo yung," I reminded him. "We always trade."

"I feel adventurous tonight. Why don't you try something new, too?"

"No, thanks, I'll just stick with what I know is good."

Sharon, looking tranquil and noncommittal, let a slight smile slip and then turned to Dad. "Where *is* their confidence in us?" she asked when the waiter left. "They brought us silverware without our even asking for it!"

Dad leaned back in his chair and laughed. "They must be good judges of character."

Sharon laid her silverware to one side. "Now, that

is a defeatist attitude. It's perfectly simple. Look, like this." She held her chopsticks in her fingers and wiggled the top one.

"We'll be here all night if Dad tries to eat that way," said Phyllis.

Dad took up the challenge. "My own daughter!" he lamented, laughing again.

"Look, hold the bottom one still and guide the top with your first finger," Sharon instructed. Phyllis tried using hers and goaded Al into trying, too. I was surrounded by laughter and flailing sticks. Disconsolately, I dumped sugar into my tea and stirred it with one chopstick.

"You can't eat tea with them," Dad quipped.

I scowled. "I'll eat the old-fashioned way."

"She means she'll *stick* to her fork!" said Al.

Everyone—except me—thought that was a great pun.

Dad, having practiced pinching napkins and a flower from the vase, which he delivered to Sharon, ate his whole meal with his chopsticks. Phyllis and Al, after a couple of sloppy attempts, reverted to their forks.

Phyllis ate gobs of fried rice, and Al said that if he hadn't already decided to be a dentist, he would open a restaurant like this. He wondered if it would be all right to add pizza to the Tea House menu, though. I'm not sure which would scare me more—having Al fix my teeth or my dinner.

Dad laughed heartily at the slightest joke, and his laughter, rolling like waves across the table, drew the others in. His eyes swept over me, and I managed a false smile to satisfy him. I had never seen him so happy.

The happier they became, the more lonely I felt. There had not been such gaiety since before my mother got sick.

When we finished eating, Dad asked for another pot of tea. The waiter brought it and a plate of fortune cookies. I closed my eyes and picked one out. I cracked it open and slipped the little tag out.

" 'A time for venturing out,' " I read. "That must mean the workshop, Dad."

He just smiled. "What does yours say, Sharon?"

She opened one. "A bright future."

This time Dad laughed. "Very good! Tea, tea everyone!" He filled all our cups and raised his in a toast. "This is a very special moment in my life. A moment I hope we will all look back on with the fondest of memories." He looked at me. Then he took Sharon's hand. Her freckles shone in the lantern light. "I have asked Sharon to be my wife and she has consented. We're getting married this September!"

I suppose I had guessed that was what the evening was about, but I had rejected it. He wouldn't go that far, I had told myself. He said he wasn't trying to replace Mom, but what was this? I was furious.

Phyllis was gushing, "Oh, that's wonderful." She

grabbed Sharon's free hand and squeezed it as if she were a girl friend who'd just announced her engagement.

Sharon, her hands outstretched to Dad and Phyllis, was radiant. And Dad and Al were smiling, smiling. Inside me, there was a voice screaming, "No!"

I clunked my teacup loudly into its little saucer and fled to the ladies' room. Dad lurched out of his chair and called my name. I heard the reveling turn to confusion behind me.

There were a few moments of solitude in which I leaned my head against the cool tile wall and tried to collect my thoughts. Then Sharon walked in.

"Carrie?"

"Please leave me alone."

"I'd like to talk with you."

"Go away. I have nothing to say to you."

"Look, Carrie, I know this is hard on you. There will be a lot of changes for everybody. But it'd be easier if we could talk about it."

I studied the floor tiles. If she thought she could patch everything up with a few words, she was crazy. "I wish you'd stay out of my life. Everything was fine at our house until you came."

"I don't want to make you miserable, Carrie, but I can't go away. My life is involved, too. I love your father."

Something inside me revolted. I wanted to run and run and scream my lungs out. I wheeled around and ducked into one of the stalls, latching the door. "Can't I please use the bathroom in peace!" I shouted.

There was a moment of silence. I stood shivering with anger and frustration.

"Well," said Sharon in a tense, controlled voice, "I'm going to keep trying, Carrie. I love your dad and there's nothing you can do or say to stop that." Sharon's sandaled feet disappeared out the bathroom door.

When I came out of the bathroom, Dad had paid the bill and they were all outside, waiting to get into the car. As we drove home, I glanced at him. His face was a mask. Sharon, Phyllis and Al all carefully avoided looking at me.

CHAPTER

6

The next morning, I awoke with the thought of Dad's marriage to Sharon. I could just see the wedding: they'd probably wear jogging clothes and have the ceremony at the high school track. The ushers would all dress like referees. There'd be badminton birdees instead of flowers, and we'd all throw golf tees instead of rice.

What was Dad thinking of, I wondered for the millionth time. If he was afraid to have another pet, how could he possibly have another wife? Suppose Sharon got cancer like Mom?

Maybe he thought I needed a mother. Well, I didn't. I wondered if Sharon would make me get rid of the picture of Mom in my room. Maybe she'd find Mom's things in the attic and throw them out one day while I was at school.

I sat up in bed and looked at the clock: 10 A.M. The rectangle of sky I could see through my window was a hazy gray white, and there was a cool, moist smell of a summer rain in the making.

Dad would have left for work a couple of hours ago, but Phyllis had the day off. I went down to the kitchen to get a banana and then went back up to stand just inside Phyllis's door. She was sitting at her sewing machine, opening the seams of the white uniform she wore at the nursing home.

She glanced up at me. "Good morning."

"Hiya." I peeled my banana down halfway, wondering how much Phyllis had learned of my little scene with Sharon. "I was thinking," I said, "do you remember those ice-cream sundaes Mom used to make?"

"Sure. They were fabulous."

"We had them a lot."

"Every Friday night. It was like a little party, remember?"

"Yeah."

Phyllis carefully put the seams together and laid the fabric on the sewing machine. She clamped the presser foot down on the very edge of the material.

"Sharon would never do that," I said.

"Why not?"

"Huh! If it was Sharon, we'd have had melon balls in carrot juice!"

Phyllis laughed. "I don't think she's that diet-crazy. She's sure a lot different from Mom, though."

"Yeah. I don't see why Dad likes her. I can't stand her."

"Carrie, she's really a nice person, if you'd open your eyes long enough to see it."

"Don't you miss Mom at all?"

Phyllis gave me a sharp look. "Of course I do. I'll always miss Mom. But it doesn't mean Dad has to live alone for the rest of his life. And it doesn't mean we have to hate any woman he cares about."

I bit off a piece of my banana. Phyllis stepped on the pedal and the machine began to hum. Her round face was taut with concentration. Outside, the sky had turned to steely gray. There was a single crack of thunder and then the rain started pattering down against the house.

Phyllis rose to close the window. "What happened between you and Sharon in the ladies' room last night?"

"Didn't she tell you all about it? I bet I was a great topic for all of you."

The corners of Phyllis's mouth turned down. "No, she didn't tell me. She wouldn't do that. She's too decent." She plunked herself down at the sewing machine and set it to whirring again.

"I don't know why you think she's so great," I grumbled. "She's busting up our whole family."

Phyllis stopped the machine again, its needle standing like a single fang waiting to bite into the material. "You think you're the center of it all! Why don't you think of Dad one time!" She drew in her breath sharply. "Carrie, you make me so mad. Go do something. I'm not supposed to talk to you about last night."

"Why not?"

"Dad's orders." She paused. "But I think it was Sharon's idea. You're lucky, too. It's obvious you're going to be a brat about this whole thing, but Sharon's hoping you'll come around if people don't bother you."

I crossed my arms. "Well, I won't."

"You're all heart, Carrie. This is a new start for Dad. You should be happy for him."

"I'm so happy I could scream! You think I'm trying to be in the center, but nobody's thinking about me at all."

"But this is good for you, too. You'll have someone to take care of you, someone to pitch in with the chores and help you with your homework."

"Who needs it? We've always managed fine."

"Carrie, I'm eighteen, remember. I won't be around forever. I have my own life to lead, but I'll feel a lot better knowing there's somebody here for you two."

"Dad and I can manage."

"And what about Sharon?" Phyllis went on. "She's a person. She's got feelings. Here she is, thirty-four years old and never married—"

"Yeah. Because nobody else could stand her."

"No, because she never met a guy worth marrying. Not everybody's as lucky as me, to meet someone when they're fourteen. So she finally meets a really nice guy—our dad—and some kid does her best to mess it up. Think how that must feel!"

"I'm not 'some kid'—I'm that nice guy's daughter!"

"Then I'd think," Phyllis said pointedly, "you'd be a better sport about it."

I turned away in disgust. "She even has you talking like a jock!"

Sharon came over again that night, and since Dad was delayed by a doctor's appointment, Phyllis entertained her. The two of them settled down on the living-room sofa. Phyllis began reading to Sharon from one of her supermarket magazines that had an article on marrying a man who had been married before. I passed by the room a couple of times on my way to the kitchen and overheard them talking.

"I don't think Dad will have a lot of those problems," Phyllis said. "He's pretty flexible."

"You must have put a lot of thought into marriage," said Sharon. "I understand you and Al are serious."

"We've gone together for four years, but we haven't come to the big decision like you and Dad."

It was funny—each one wanted to talk about the other's romance.

Dad and I didn't get any time alone together until the next evening. I would have gladly waited longer to hear his reaction to the dinner fiasco. To my surprise, he came with an apology.

I was in the kitchen, up to my elbows in dishwater, when he ambled in. "Carrie, I wanted to let you know I regret announcing the wedding at the restaurant the other night," he said.

My heart started beating fast. Was he about to say it was all off?

"I know you're having trouble with all this and a restaurant just wasn't the place."

I held a plate under the running water, staring at the water swirling off of it.

Dad leaned one elbow on the counter in order to see my face better. "It's just that it was an important moment for me, a joyous one, and I wanted to share it. At the time I didn't stop to think what a bomb it was to drop on you."

"S'okay," I lied. I always let the dishes drip dry, but this time I turned away from Dad to get the dish towel off the refrigerator door. I dried that dish top, bottom and edges.

"You're still upset, I guess."

I shrugged and found some dishes on the kitchen table to gather up. I just wasn't up to another scene, and that's all I could see happening if I opened my mouth.

"Well, I guess you're not ready to talk about it. But when you are—"

"Okay."

He hesitated a moment and then left. I set the dishes in the sink and went out to sit on the back step, breathing in the night air.

* * *

Being home had become unbearable. Phyllis was wildly excited about the wedding. Every time Sharon was over, Phyllis latched onto her, trying to get in on the planning. She dragged Al around with her everywhere. I think she was hoping he'd get in the marrying mood, too.

I was more determined than ever to go to the workshop. In two and a half weeks, I had brought my savings up to seventy-four dollars. The workshop began August 13. That left me five weeks. I might just make it.

Bridget had become part of the crew painting scenery at the Young People's Theater, which the university sponsored. That helped me. I didn't have to decide whether to go off somewhere with her or work, since she was busy so much.

I was working steadily. Grace gave my name to a friend of hers, Mrs. Diago, who wanted me to take her clothes to the laundromat. Another lady, who had seen my card at the shopping center, asked me to water her plants while she was out of town.

And Grace was great at finding jobs for me—housecleaning, painting and helping set up the new greenhouse. I went over nearly every afternoon after the art class, and she usually had enough work to keep me busy until dinnertime. She said it was all getting a bit too much for her to handle, but I was beginning to wonder if she wasn't just trying to find ways for me to earn money. I would have worked for her whether she paid me or not, though. I was glad to get out of the house.

On Thursday when I arrived, Grace was sitting on the steps of the kitchen porch. Her face was strangely pale and I ran to meet her. "Grace, is something wrong?"

She sighed and invited me in. On the counter beside the stove lay a partially burned cloth. Vegetable soup was splashed everywhere—on the wall, across the counter and stove and dripping onto the floor. A little blob of cooked tomato slithered off the counter edge.

I sucked in my breath. "What happened?"

"It was so stupid of me," she said in a strangely passive tone. "I laid my apron down on the counter. The burner was lit. I left the room for a moment and it caught."

Her blue eyes were damp and fear shivered through me. She seemed so helpless.

"I'll clean it up for you, Grace, don't worry."

"I picked up the pot of soup and threw it on the fire. It was all I could think of to do. The curtain was starting to catch, too."

"You're not hurt, are you?"

"No. The soup wasn't hot yet. Carrie, for a moment I didn't do anything—just stood there thinking, 'Oh, my God, the house is on fire.' "

We stood looking at the vegetables clinging to the wall above the counter. The soup spread everywhere.

"Let me get you some lemonade," I said. "Why don't you rest in the living room while I take care of this."

She nodded, letting me help her get settled there. Then I began sponging down the walls and dropping the vegetables into the trash. I had the job about half done when she came back.

"Make some room for me to help," she said.

"You don't have to," I said. "I don't mind, really."

"I'm all right now, Carrie. Run downstairs and fetch the mop for me."

I looked at her. Her eyes were clear and sharp once more and the paleness had gone from her face.

"I'm not going to let this episode end with my acting like a foolish old woman." She winked.

I grinned back at her with relief and ran down for the mop.

When we were finished, we had some apple cake she had baked that morning and lemonade.

"My dad is going to marry Sharon," I said.

"You don't look very happy about it."

"I'm not. I don't see why he wants to get married again. You wouldn't do that, would you, Grace?"

She took a moment before answering. "No, I don't think I would. But your father is quite a bit younger than I. Though after today"—she smiled—"I'm wondering if I shouldn't have a husband to look after me."

I chewed my thumbnail. I knew Grace was older, but Dad was no teen-ager.

"Tell me about Sharon," she said.

"There's nothing much to tell. She's a health nut and a jock. She runs a sports store."

"What sort of person is she?" asked Grace. "Is she friendly? Does she like kids and pets?"

She was friendly, I admitted to myself. And she seemed to like most everything. "I don't know," I said, looking away. "I don't talk to her much. She butts in a lot. Did you decide to paint the bathroom lavender or green?"

"Green," said Grace, graciously allowing me to change the subject. "Are you ready to start?"

"Uh huh." We didn't talk about Sharon or Dad anymore that day.

On Friday, after I'd worked for Grace every spare minute that week, she said, "We ought to fix up a room for you here, Carrie."

My eyes widened. "Could we really?"

She laughed. "I was joking, honey. I love having you here, but doesn't your family miss you?"

"No. Dad and Phyllis are working most of the time, and when they're not working, they're busy with their romances."

"Have you gotten a chance to know Sharon any better?"

"Not yet. But I suppose I'll have to when she's living with us."

Grace thoughtfully polished her glasses with her handkerchief and replaced them. "Your father may seem too busy, but I'll bet he needs you," she said. "When something important happens, people need to share it."

When I got home that evening, Dad was sitting quietly in the living room. The TV was silent. What Grace said flashed through my mind. For an instant I wondered if he needed me. Then I saw my sketch pad on his lap. I realized with a jolt that I had sat in that chair sketching last night while he was out and had forgotten to put the pad away. "Oh, hi, Dad," I said casually. "I guess I left that laying around, huh? Maybe I'll clean up my room tonight. Get everything organized."

Dad flipped open the pad to the picture of Sharon and looked up at me. "I didn't know you were drawing this sort of thing."

I felt like snatching the pad out of his hand. Why was he looking through it anyway? Sometimes I showed him my drawings or he'd ask to see them. But he never just started looking through them. Now, suddenly, he was snooping. I shrugged and kept my voice calm.

"Oh, that—that's just a joke. From a new cartoon show on TV. 'Featherhead,' it's called."

"It's supposed to be Sharon, isn't it, Carrie?"

"Yes, sir."

There was silence. The clock's ticking sounded like the drumbeat in a death march.

Dad carefully folded the sketch pad shut. He

stared at the cover for a long time. "Carrie, we haven't been seeing much of each other lately, have we?"

"No, sir, not too much."

"How would you like to grab a hamburger and go miniature golfing tonight?"

"Yes, sir. I'd like that."

I couldn't believe it. We went to my favorite restaurant, the Dixie Diner. We sat on stools at the counter where we could see the hamburgers sizzling on the grill. The orange-punch tank was right beside me. The punch shot up like a little geyser and streamed down the sides of the tank, making me thirsty just to see it.

While we were waiting for our food, Dad sat drumming his fingers lightly on his folded arms. I was worried that he might start talking to me about Sharon. He seemed to be thinking hard.

"Dad, do you have to go to school to run a diner?"

He turned on his stool to look at me, the look of concentration draining away. "No. It helps if you have some training in business if you're going to actually manage it, but you can learn it on the job."

"Didn't you say you had a diner once?"

He chuckled. "No, I worked in one in high school. I could have gone on to manage one, though. I worked the counter, washed dishes, mopped, ran the cash register—even flipped a few hamburgers. That's the great thing about a job like this—they fit you in where you're needed and you learn a lot of different jobs."

I began to relax. Maybe we really were going to have fun and not talk about a lot of serious junk.

"Didn't you think it would be fun to have your own diner?"

"Oh, sure. Sometimes. My boss thought quite highly of me and wanted to train me as an assistant manager. I could've had a diner of my own eventually—it was a chain."

The food arrived. I had ordered a hamburger with a big coil of onion on it, and I loaded it with so much ketchup that it squeezed out over my fingers. "You must have been good at your job."

Dad pushed a protruding piece of turkey back into his club sandwich with the tip of his knife. "I guess I was," he said modestly. "It's more a matter of hard work. If you throw yourself into your work—whatever it is—you can usually succeed."

It was a perfect opening for me to explain that that was exactly what I was trying to do with art. Throw myself into it. Practice, practice. Try to learn all I could—even going to that recreation class. And—most important—not let any special opportunities like the workshop go by. But I just bit into my hamburger. If I started talking about the workshop, he'd start talking about Sharon and marriage.

After we finished our sandwiches, we ordered dessert. The pies and cakes were all displayed in a glass case on the counter. It took me about ten minutes to decide, but finally I asked for pecan pie.

Then we went to the miniature golf course. I used to think that course was the greatest thing. It starts out easy, with just turns in the green and ramps you putt the ball up. Toward the end you have to hit the ball through a windmill and then a clown's mouth that opens and closes. If you miss and hit the clown's nose, a buzzer goes off and everyone laughs. I used to think that was a great joke when I was a kid and I always tried to hit the nose.

On the first few greens, Dad and I talked about what a nice night it was and how the course had gotten battered-looking since we'd last come there. On the fourth green, he said, "This is fun, isn't it?"

"Yes," I said. I set my ball on the rubber mat and gave it a sharp crack with my club. It shot up the green, rattled around the metal curlicue and came to rest a few inches from the hole. "But it seems a lot easier now."

"You know, when Sharon and I are married, there will be just another person to join in the fun."

I tapped the ball into the hole and retrieved it, and we walked to the next green.

"Sharon likes you and Phyllis," Dad went on. He shot his ball over the moat with the alligators painted on the bottom and into the hole with one putt. Then he stood at the other end of the green and waited for me.

"That's nice," I said. I hit my ball into the moat and got a penalty. Dad always used to say, "Watch those alligators!" when I went after my ball, but this time his face looked strained. I could tell he was trying to think of what to say next. I should have known at the diner that things couldn't continue to go smoothly.

"I think if you gave Sharon a chance, you'd like her, too."

"I'm sure she's real nice, Dad."

"No, I mean it, Carrie."

The next green had a narrow passage you had to shoot through. On the green with the bent tunnel, Dad tried again.

"Carrie, Sharon and I will be married very soon. We can't live with a lot of bad feelings in the house."

"I don't see why you have to get married. Why can't you just be friends?"

"It's not the same, honey."

"Dad, don't you wonder why she's never married? Doesn't it make you wonder what's wrong with her?"

"There's nothing wrong with Sharon but a spirit of adventure. You should appreciate that, Carrie. She didn't spend her life shopping for a husband. She was raised in Baton Rouge and went to school in Grambling. Then she went to a ski resort in Vermont and later worked for the recreation department in Ohio.

"After she got her fill of moving around she came back to Louisiana and took a job with the Good Sports Shop." Dad marked our scores down on the card and gave me a slap on the back. "Carrie, it looks like all this talk of equality for women has been lost on you," he said, attempting humor. "Marriage is no longer the primary goal for all women."

I frowned. Since when was Dad a champion of women's rights, I wondered. We moved up to the eighth green. The windmill turned, blocking off the passageway underneath. Timing was important. Dad watched the propeller and putted, slipping his ball through just as the blade came down. "Anyway, Carrie, I think you'll enjoy having a woman in the house. Someone you can talk to. Especially someone as interesting as Sharon."

I chopped my ball three times and still couldn't get it through. Finally I picked it up and carried it to the next green. "Penalize me. I hate that windmill. Your turn, Dad." I chewed my lip.

Dad set his ball on the mat, glancing up at me. He raised his club to swing. "Look, Dad," I burst out. "I don't want someone to talk to. I used to be able to talk to you. Besides, I still love Mom, even if you don't. I don't like Sharon!"

Dad swept his arms down. His club cracked against the ball and it flew over the green and smacked the clown's nose. The buzzer sounded, and everybody looked at him and hooted.

Dad snatched up his ball and headed for the cashier. "Let's go," he said gruffly.

When we got to the car, he held the door open for me. "It's not a question of loving one or the other, Carrie. I thought you understood that. I never stopped loving your mother, but I love Sharon now, too. One has nothing to do with the other."

"I think one has everything to do with the other! How can you love them both? Sharon is nothing like Mom!"

"Sharon keeps asking me what she's doing wrong with you—what she can do to make you like her. I don't know what to tell her. She's as nice as she can be to you, and all you do is give her the cold shoulder. Why can't you accept her like Phyllis does? What do you want from her?"

"I don't want anything from her! I just don't want her!" I jumped into the car, scowling.

"How can you be so selfish!" Dad shouted.

He slammed my door shut, walked around to the driver's seat and started up the car. A picture of Mom flashed into my mind, and I held it there firmly. One day, I told myself, Dad would be glad he gave Sharon up. Or he would wish he had.

We drove a couple of blocks and Dad pulled over. "It's been four years since you mother died, Carrie. She is a very special memory for me and always will be. However, I believe she wouldn't ask me to isolate myself for the rest of my life, and I think I knew her better than you did."

He waited a moment, but I didn't respond.

"I'm not asking you to forget your mother. I trust you'll always remember her. And I'm not asking you to love Sharon—only to be decent to her and give her a chance. But understand this—I love her and I will marry her. I guess you'll just have to get used to that."

Dad started driving again. I rolled down the window, closed my eyes and let the wind blow on my face. We didn't speak the rest of the way.

CHAPTER
7

I'd been going to the art class for a week and a half now and found I actually enjoyed it. I didn't talk to the little kids and Mr. Stewart didn't try to lump us together. I found my own projects to work on, and when Mr. Stewart came around, he usually had something helpful to say. I think he liked my work. Dad seemed pleased that I was going, and I was glad that I was doing something that made him happy.

Grace asked again to see my sketches, but I couldn't think of a thing I had done that I wanted to show her. There were plenty of cartoons, of course, but I felt like drawing something especially for her. Something serious and difficult.

Every morning at class I tried to draw something to show her. I tried to draw my mother. My most recent memories of her were the ones when she was sick and in pain. I tried to recall earlier ones, but my memory was not as sharp and clear as I needed it to be. When I tried to copy the photograph I'd brought from home, it turned out to be flat and lifeless.

Frustrated, I turned my thoughts to Toby. I thought of how cute he used to look when he'd flop down at my feet with his chin on his paws and roll his eyes up at me. I thought of how sleek and fast he was when he first sighted a cat and leaped after it. But when I tried to put those things on paper, that drawing, too, looked dull and flat. It could have been any dog, and it made me mad that I'd missed the feeling.

In the end I drew cartoons of the nine-year-olds flailing their brushes around, with paint dripping from their elbows. Mr. Stewart looked at the drawings and tugged his moustache. "You know, you're very talented, Carrie. I'd like to see you try something of a serious nature."

"I only do cartoons," I told him.

Finally, because there was nothing else, I showed Grace the pictures of the kids at class. "Cartoons," I said, disparagingly. "It's all I have right now."

There were five of them and Grace looked at each one carefully, her smile growing and growing. Then she spread them all out on the table and laughed. "They're wonderful!" she exclaimed. "That must be some class!"

"Yeah." I grinned. "It's just about that bad, too."

I was disappointed not to have achieved what I wanted, but still, her reaction made me happy.

She looked at the pictures again and shook her head. "I didn't know you did cartoons. You never let me see the comic side of you before."

"It wasn't what I wanted to show you. I wanted to do something important."

"Cartoons are important. People need to laugh, to see humor in their situations."

I knew she was right, but there was a layer beneath that held the hurt and the love. That was what I had wanted to reach.

"I guess," I said. "But I wanted to do something realistic. Something to do with serious feelings."

Grace nodded. "Feelings can be so elusive. It's hard enough to understand our feelings sometimes, let alone portray them."

The next night an exhibit of the summer students' artwork began at Tulane University. For once, neither Bridget nor I had something planned, so we were able to go together. We were passing by Grace's house on our way when she leaned out her kitchen door and called to me.

"Carrie! I could use your help if you're free."

Running up the walk, I noticed Grace was in her bare feet. She helped open the kitchen door. "Better look before you step in."

We peered in. The floor was covered with about an inch of water. A plumber was picking up his tools.

"What happened?" I asked.

"A pipe burst. I was in the garden and didn't know it until it had flooded the place. It's going to be quite a job to get all this water up—"

"We'll be glad to help, won't we, Bridget?"

"Sure."

"Wonderful. There's a mop and bucket in the cellar."

Bridget kicked off her sandals and waded in, while I ran home for another mop. Soon we were all hard at work: Bridget and I mopping up and Grace drying off all the bottles and boxes she had stored under the sink.

"What a mess!" Bridget exclaimed. "I'll bet this got under your linoleum."

"It may have."

"It probably ruined it. You'll probably have to get a new floor."

"Perhaps."

Bridget wrung out her mop and squinted up at Grace. "Aren't you mad? My mom would be absolutely livid."

"Well, it isn't how I'd hoped to spend my evening," Grace admitted.

"And all the money it's costing you," Bridget persisted. "And the waste of time. That's what'd get my mom. She'd be yelling about how they don't make pipes right anymore."

"Bridget's mom is a social worker," I explained. "She believes in getting her feelings out."

Grace smiled. She was down on her knees now,

pushing water out of the emptied cabinet. The hem of her dress was soaked. "This isn't the sort of thing that stirs me up. If I let this make me angry, then I'd have two problems—a flooded kitchen and an angry me."

I shot a glance at Bridget and caught her perplexed look. I grinned. Mrs. Calloway should have a talk with Grace sometime.

The next morning was the last art class. Grace wasn't home when I went by that afternoon. Carrot slinked out from behind a bush and leaped into my arms. Then he cried and jumped down to go lie on the porch. I peered in through the windows, but it was dark inside.

That evening Dad told me he had been talking with Mrs. Pendleton, and she needed someone to take care of her dog while she was on vacation. I went over to see her.

"Hello, Carolyn," she said, standing in her doorway. "I've been meaning to mention what a fine young lady you're growing into."

"Thank you, ma'am," I said. "My father said you needed someone to take care of your dog."

"Yes. Your father—he's such a lovely man. It's nice he's found himself a new wife, don't you think? A new mother for you girls. A shame it couldn't have happened sooner, but better late than—"

"Yes'm. About your dog—"

"Oh, Max! Herbert and I are going to Hawaii—

imagine, after all these years, we've scrimped and saved and finally have enough to go—"

Trying to talk with Mrs. Pendleton was wearying. For a moment, I wondered if the job was worth it. "When would you like me to start, Mrs. Pendleton?"

She laughed self-consciously. "You know, it slipped my mind, I'm so embarrassed. We're leaving tomorrow and I've made no special plans for Max. Could you, dear—"

"Yes'm. I can start right away."

"Splendid. I'll be sure to tell your father what a helpful young lady you are. Come around the back with me and I'll show you Max's food and things. I think it would be nice if you walked Max tonight so he can become accustomed to you. He's a little shy with strangers, you know."

As soon as we turned the corner of the house, Max bent his head down and gave a low growl. Mrs. Pendleton handed me a box of dog biscuits so I could bribe him into liking me. Max was a bow-legged boxer and about the ugliest dog I'd ever seen. I held a biscuit out to him. He inched forward, snapped it up, retreated and growled again. This went on for about twenty biscuits. Finally, he decided to make friends. I guess his stomach was full.

I clipped the leash on Max's collar and led him down the street. We stopped every few feet so he could sniff me again. I could tell ours would be a trying relationship.

I figured if Grace had been out to the store that afternoon, she'd be back by evening, so I walked Max by her house, but it was still dark.

She must have gone away for a while, I thought. But that didn't make sense. I saw her every day. She would tell me if she was going. And why wouldn't she take Carrot?

After I penned up Max, I brought Carrot some milk and sardines. That was Friday. On Saturday night, Sharon came for dinner again. Phyllis cooked this time so we had normal food—fried chicken, mashed potatoes and green beans.

Grace still hadn't come home and I was worried. I'd checked her house a dozen times that day. Something was wrong. Carrot looked worried, too.

"Dad," I said, "I haven't seen Grace since Thursday."

"Oh? Did she go out of town?"

"I don't know."

"Who's Grace?" Sharon asked.

"An elderly woman Carrie's been working for."

"I haven't just been working for her," I protested. "She's my friend. I can't figure out why she's not home. She didn't say anything about going on a trip."

Phyllis smiled condescendingly. "Older people don't like to be held accountable to children," she said. "Pass the gravy, please."

"She may be older, but I'm still her friend. I've

seen Grace practically every day this summer, and suddenly she's gone without a word," I told Dad.

"That does seem strange," Sharon said. "You must be worried."

"Yeah. I am."

"She lives all alone? No family nearby?"

I met Sharon's eyes and felt uneasy. I wanted to keep my feelings private, but I wanted reassurance even more. "Near as I can tell, she doesn't have anybody. Just her cat. And he's still home."

"I wonder if she's sick. Maybe just not answering her door."

"No, she's not home at all. There are never any lights on," I said. "Besides, she once told me she never even gets a headache."

Dad glanced at Sharon. "Carrie's told me about the work Mrs. Stebbins has been doing. She is remarkably robust." He turned to me. "Maybe she had to go out of town suddenly. She might have a sick relative to visit. I'll bet she'll be back by Sunday evening."

I kept checking Grace's house all day Sunday. I went on a picnic with the Calloways for a while, but I couldn't stand not knowing if she'd come home, and I walked back early. She still wasn't home, but Carrot had gotten stranded up in the tree again. I hauled him down in the basket. After I put a sardine inside, it worked pretty well.

No one was home at my house either, so I got Max

and took him for a walk. Max tried to chase Carrot and I had to wrap the leash around a tree to hold him back. I decided not to walk Max by there anymore. Carrot was nicer than Max any day.

When I came in from Max's walk, Dad was home. He was clearing the old clothes out of his closet to make room for Sharon's stuff. He looked startled when I walked in. He stuffed an old suit into a bag for Goodwill, then sat down on the edge of his bed and looked at me for a moment. His eyes were serious and sad.

"Carrie," he said at last, "your friend Grace has had a heart attack."

CHAPTER
8

It was just as well that the art class was over, because I had no desire to draw anything. Several days passed aimlessly. When Bridget called, I told her I was busy. The days were long and lonely, and somehow, I wanted them that way.

Dad said Grace was in intensive care, that she wasn't allowed to do anything but lie around and that only immediate family could visit her there. I had made her a card with a cartoon of Carrot and me standing by a window, pining away. Inside I said how much I missed her and that I would look after Carrot. There had been no reply.

My chief activity was feeding and walking Max. One morning I was hanging on to the leather strap of Max's leash, letting him tug me along whichever way he wanted. Max sat down abruptly and looked at me with his grumpy, heavy-jowled face. I jiggled his leash to get him going again. I wasn't ready to go back to the house.

A voice interrupted my thoughts.

"Mornin', Carrie." It was Mr. Keager, the man who lived at the end of our street. He was sitting on his porch with a cast on his leg.

"Mornin', sir."

"You wouldn't know a boy around here that wants a job mowing the lawn, would you?"

"No, sir. Gary Thomas is in summer camp and Tom Wallace is working at the gas station this year."

Mr. Keager was bending a coat hanger out straight. He poked it down under his cast and gently scratched. "Summer's a bad time for a broken leg," he said. "This cast is hot and itches like the devil."

"How'd you break your leg?"

His stepson, Bobby, who had been listening at the door, stepped out on the porch. "He was riding in the car and somebody ran into him—smack!" Bobby slammed his fist into his hand. "It was Mama's car, too."

I looked at the lawn. The grass was ankle-deep—not so hard to mow, but it would be soon. Max was straining to move on, but I caught his collar in two hands and held him. "I can mow your lawn, Mr. Keager."

Mr. Keager shifted in his chair. "You sure? Takes a lot of muscle power."

"Sure. I do ours. I'll just pen Max up and come back and do it."

"Well . . . well, I thank you, then. Bobby's only six; he can't push the mower yet. Here, Bobby, come get the key to the shed and open it so Carrie can get the mower."

When I got back, Bobby was on the sidewalk playing with his trucks. "Mr. Dad went inside to cool his heels," Bobby said, as I pulled the lawn mower out of the shed.

"Oh." I gripped the mower, mentally marking off a section, and pushed.

Bobby sat on the sidewalk, his arms clasped around his knees, watching. Finally he hitched up his shorts and sauntered over to me.

"You better do a good job," he said, "or Mr. Dad won't pay you."

"I'll do it good, Bobby. Don't worry."

"Mr. Dad is mean."

"That so?"

"Yeah. He's not my real father, you know."

I wiped my brow quickly and leaned into the mower. "I know, Bobby. You tell me that every time I see you."

Bobby stuck his jaw out. "They try to make me call him Dad, but I won't. I call him Mr. Dad."

"He doesn't look mean to me."

"Oh yeah? He's so mean my real father sent me

money to see him and Mr. Dad said no. I was gonna fly in a plane."

I'd never flown anywhere, and I sure couldn't picture Dad letting me take a plane alone when I was six. I didn't say this to Bobby, though. I knew it would just make him mad.

"Mr. Dad is so mean," Bobby went on, "I have to hide my picture of my real dad or he'll put a curse on him. Mr. Dad's got evil powers, you know."

"Oh, Bobby, that's dumb, that's really dumb." I pushed the lawn mower around the back of the house to get away from him. Suddenly it occurred to me that if I were six, I might be saying those things about Sharon.

"Yeah, well, I bet he doesn't pay you anything!" Bobby shouted. "I bet he laughs in your face!"

I tried to imagine Mr. Keager laughing after I did all that work. He'd always been nice to me. It was too bad Bobby couldn't see what a nice man he was.

I stopped mowing for a moment, looking across the crisscross of fence tops behind the house. Bobby was so angry, he didn't make sense when he talked about his stepfather. And he was a pain to be around. Probably Dad and Phyllis were thinking I was a dumb, bratty kid, just as I was thinking about Bobby. I got an uneasy feeling in the pit of my stomach. Maybe they were right. Maybe I was too angry to see what a nice woman Sharon was.

I gave the lawn mower my full strength. Getting a stepparent was different for me, I reasoned. Bobby was a little kid. He hadn't had all the years I'd had getting used to living with just family.

When I finished the lawn, I knocked on the screen door. In a moment, Mr. Keager hobbled out on crutches. He looked at the lawn. "That's a good job, Carrie. I thank you." He reached in his pocket and handed me two dollars. "Does that seem fair?"

"Yes, sir. It didn't take that long."

"Well, you earned it. I'll be in this cast for a while, so if you're willing, in a week or so—"

"Yes, sir. I'll come back." I stuffed the bills into my pocket. "Thank you, Mr. Keager."

As I left, Bobby stuck his tongue out at me.

It had been several days since I'd seen Carrot. I went over to Grace's and started poking around the bushes, calling him. Suddenly Grace's door opened a crack and a woman's head popped out.

"What are you doing, child?"

For a minute, I was too surprised to speak, and I just stared. She looked vaguely like Grace, but her hair was stiff and blue and her cheeks were rouged.

"Uh—I'm looking for Gr—Mrs. Stebbins's cat, Carrot, ma'am," I said.

"I've got that little old cat inside, child. What do you want with it?"

"Well, since Mrs. Stebbins is in the hospital, I've been looking after it."

The woman stepped out on the porch, carefully

closing the screen door behind her. "That's mighty nice, honey, but I'll tend to Mrs. Stebbins's cat. I'm her sister, Mrs. Appleby."

"Yes'm," I said and started away. Then I looked back. "Will she be all right—Mrs. Stebbins, I mean?"

"Why, surely," Mrs. Appleby trilled. "She surely will."

A couple of weeks passed before Grace was moved to the regular ward and I was allowed to see her. Dad sent me off with a warning. "Don't expect her to look as she did. She's been through a lot. She'll probably be very tired."

"But you'd be amazed how well people can recuperate from heart attacks," Phyllis added. "It just takes some time."

"I just can't get away from the office today," Dad said. "Wouldn't you rather wait until tonight when I could go with you?"

"No. I've been waiting long enough. I want to go now."

"Phyllis, maybe you could take off?"

Phyllis looked doubtful. "I don't know. They're short-handed at the nursing home and some of those patients really depend on me."

"Look," I said, suddenly feeling irritable. "I know people don't feel good when they're sick. I don't need anyone to go with me."

But when I stepped into the slick, clean hospital

lobby, I felt a sudden panic. I was alone in a place where some people were fighting for their lives. And sometimes lost.

I pushed the thought from my mind and started down the long, brightly lit corridors. I didn't ask anyone how to get to Grace's room. I didn't want anyone asking me if I was old enough to be there. Instead, I followed the room-number signs on the walls.

A nurse wheeled a haggard woman past me. She had no legs. In the corner near the elevators, janitors leaned on their mops and joked with each other. Over the loudspeaker a voice crackled: "Dr. Lamont, report to the emergency room immediately. Dr. James wanted in surgery. Stat." I couldn't understand why Phyllis wanted to be in a place like this. It was hard enough to visit, let alone work in.

At last I spotted Grace's room number. Despite Dad's warning, I had imagined her to be the same, only lying down, with her hair a little messy, perhaps. But she was drained, like one of those lifeless drawings of mine.

A middle-aged nurse was giving her a back rub. "May I help you, dear?"

Grace's eyes drifted over to me. "Carrie," she said softly. "Mrs. Du Bois, this is my dear friend, Carrie."

Mrs. Du Bois smiled broadly and nodded. Then she turned back to Grace. "Would you like me to leave you with your visitor, Mrs. Stebbins?"

"Yes, that would be nice, thank you."

Mrs. Du Bois rustled out, her rubber soles squeaking on the shining floor.

Grace held out her hand, and I went over and put my hand in hers. I was afraid to sit on the edge of the bed. I stood there awkwardly, looking down at her and trying to think of something to say.

"Your sister's taking care of Carrot," I said at last.

Grace nodded. "Yes. That's good."

"I didn't know you had a sister."

"Yes, just the one."

"I was surprised. You never mentioned her. She seems a lot different than you."

Grace smoothed a wrinkle out of her sheet. "We seldom see each other. We've never been close," she said.

I was sure I was one of the few people close to Grace since Edward. I knew she had other friends, but I felt a special bond between us. Perhaps because we had both lost someone special. But Grace knew how to get up and start again. She wouldn't let this heart attack keep her down. She'd bounce back, like she did after Edward died. That was just the way she was.

"Would you like me to bring you some chocolate?"

She smiled weakly. "Thank you, but I'm not allowed to have it. The doctor says I have to baby my heart."

There was a long, vacant silence. Grace closed her eyes, and I thought she was asleep. She looked so washed out in that white hospital gown. I watched her chest gently rise and fall. The sunlight filtered in through the blinds and lit up tiny particles of dust in the air. In the hallway a man was mopping and the overpowering odor of ammonia wafted in. I heard the mindless moaning of a man across the hall. My stomach churned.

Grace's eyes opened. "I'm so tired," she apologized.

"Maybe I better go."

She sighed. "Please come back, though. It's good to have a friend come by."

The next day when I arrived, Mrs. Keager and another lady were there. I had to wait until they left because only two visitors were allowed in at a time.

When I went in, I noticed a large arrangement of flowers had been placed on her night table. I had brought a prayer plant, which I'd bought at the florist's on the way over. Its broad spotted leaves opened to the sun during the day; at night they closed up like hands in prayer.

"It doesn't look like much next to that," I said, looking at the arrangement.

"It's wonderful. I've never had one before."

I put it in the window for her, so it would catch the sunlight. "You could make cuttings and grow a whole bunch of them in your greenhouse when you go home," I said.

She smiled. "Yes. That's just what I should do."

I didn't tell Dad or Phyllis how bad Grace looked. I just said that she was fine and that I didn't mind going alone to see her.

By the fourth day, however, she still looked the same. I wondered when she would come home. "In due time, Carrie," Grace said. "Don't worry." Mrs. Du Bois just smiled and said it was up to the doctor.

On the fifth morning when I came by, Mrs. Du Bois told me Grace had gone to the chapel services downstairs. She suggested I come back later. I caught the bus to my street. Maybe Bridget was home. It seemed like forever since I'd seen her, and I was tired of being alone. Bridget would understand how grim things had been lately, or try to. At least she would cheer me up.

She met me at the door. "Hi, stranger," she said. "Come on in."

Across the living room, sliding glass doors opened to the backyard. I saw Brian there, working around a blazing campfire.

"Bridget, it's ninety-two degrees out," I said. "What is Brian doing?"

"Making lunch. He just made an oven out of a potato chip can and some screening."

"Is your oven broken?"

"No. Brian's been on a self-sufficiency kick lately. He's planning to get lost in the woods for a few days."

I had to smile. Going to the Calloways' was a treat. I never knew who would be doing what. It renewed my faith in the future. The world was full of unanticipated possibilities.

We went to Bridget's room, and I flopped down on her bed.

"Okay," said Bridget. "You've kept me in suspense long enough. I'm leaving for the workshop in ten days. Can you come or not?"

"No."

"Oh, Carrie! Couldn't you raise the money?"

"Not enough." I shrugged. "They have the workshops every summer. Maybe I'll have enough next year."

"Yeah, but this is the year I'm going and that Uncle Greg offered to show us around. Why don't you ask your dad to loan you the rest?"

I rolled over on my back, lethargically watching Bridget's scrap mobile twirl in the breeze of the electric fan. "I dunno. I guess I don't care about going anymore."

Bridget sat down on the edge of the bed. "What's gotten into you?"

"It just doesn't seem important. I'm worried about Grace. Ever since she went to the hospital, all I've wanted to do is stick around and make sure she's okay."

"She's going to get better, isn't she?"

"Sure. I guess." Suddenly I wondered how I could answer that way. I didn't really know. I imagined asking her doctor and dismissed the thought. I wasn't a relative, and moreover, I was a kid.

"But she wants you to go to the workshop, right?" Bridget argued. "She helped you get the money. You could write her a letter every day. That would cheer her up."

"Yeah. But I would feel terrible. I need to be here. The afternoon my mom died I was at the movies. I hated myself for weeks for going to the movies that day."

"But Grace isn't going to die!" Bridget protested. "She's getting better, right? That's why she's not in intensive care, right?"

"Right," I said, shrinking into the past. The movie had been *The Pink Panther Strikes Again.* No one knew Mom would die that day. While she was dying, I was laughing my head off. I didn't even feel anything at the moment it happened. Dad picked me up at my friend's house afterward and told me. I cried until I could neither cry nor feel, and then I slept. When I awoke, there was not a part of me that didn't ache.

I sat up. "Bridget. Let's go for a walk."

She looked at me momentarily, then tipped her head, letting a veil of hair fall across her eyes. Then she flicked the hair away. Her hazel eyes were clear and unsearching. "Okay," she said. "Let's go down to the French Quarter. I could pick up some more paints while we're there."

I had never walked downtown, but Bridget knew the way. Our neighborhood's quiet, secluded streets gave way to the houses around Tulane. There were the sprawling, impressive mansions of deans and important professors and the crowded, broken-down apartments that housed the students. Now the campuses were mostly empty, except for a few summer students who lay out on the green with their textbooks.

The student apartments ended as abruptly as did the trees. Suddenly the streets were lined with shabby hotels and old buildings with signs that read ROOMS FOR MEN. An old man sat on the steps of one building with his head in his hands. Beside him was a paper bag wrapped around a bottle. He smelled like dirt and whiskey. I drew closer to Bridget and walked a little faster.

Finally we reached Canal Street and crossed over into the French Quarter. We didn't go down Bourbon Street, where all the bars were. We headed straight for the Café du Monde, which sat on the edge of the Quarter, across from Jackson Square. The café and a couple of praline shops were about the only places I'd ever been in the Quarter.

We ordered big powdered doughnuts and café au lait. Every time I bit into the doughnut, the powder puffed out like smoke and settled on my clothes. Overhead, the big propeller fans hummed as they spun.

When we went outside I could smell the Mississippi River behind us. Tugboats and barges rocked on the broad bed of water. I wanted to go sit on the rocks and watch the river rolling and lapping, completely unconcerned with the activities of the people around it.

But Bridget wanted me to meet her friend Leon, so we went to Jackson Square. There the street artists nearly outnumbered the pigeons. They propped their paintings up against the wrought-iron fences and set up their easels on the sidewalk. Beside their easels were stacks of paintings, each one like the one on the easel.

Leon wore a purple beret and a dry paintbrush behind one ear. He sat on a canvas stool in front of his easel.

"Hey, little artist," he said, when he saw Bridget. His hair and beard were tinged with white, but he was not an old man.

"Hiya. This is my friend, Carrie. She does cartoons."

A cluster of well-dressed people moved down the sidewalk in our direction. Leon got up and started dabbing at the half-finished painting on his easel until they passed by. Then he sat down, pushed back his beret and regarded me with interest. "Cartoons, huh? Can you do pictures of real people?"

"I guess so."

"Sure she can," said Bridget. "She can draw anybody."

"Then you could make some bread off these tourists. They love to buy funny pictures of themselves."

"Maybe you could still get the money for the workshop," Bridget suggested.

"Maybe," I said, but I knew I wouldn't do it.

"It would be good for you to get away, Carrie," said Bridget. "Grace would understand. Really."

"I can't, Bridget. I just can't go this time."

A look passed between us, and I knew Bridget understood. She might not understand all the reasons. She didn't know me when my mother died. I hadn't talked with her much about it, either. But she knew Grace was important to me. And she knew me well enough to know when to coax and when to give up.

She laid her hand on my arm. "Come on. I'll buy you a Popsicle."

We found a vendor on the corner and watched an old lady feed the pigeons while we ate our Popsicles. Then we ran through the pigeons; they rose up like a great, gray, squawking cloud. We lay in the grass, staring into the sky. We listened to two guys playing a fiddle and a guitar. A small crowd collected, and Bridget pulled me up and we did a little square dance amid the foot-stomping and hand-clapping.

Then we went to the art store for Bridget's paints.

"I'm too tired to walk back, Bridge," I told her, as we left the art store.

She nodded. "Me, too."

I looked at my watch. "Uh oh, it's six o'clock. I have to get back for dinnner." I reached into my pocket to get some bus money and realized I had spent it. Bridget had spent all but fifteen cents on the paints.

"Nobody'll be home at my place till late," she said. "Why don't you call your sister?"

Calling Phyllis for help was the last thing I wanted to do, but there didn't seem to be much choice.

She sounded annoyed when I told her. "You're in the French Quarter? Not at some bar, I hope! Wait a minute, Dad's talking to me."

I could hear muffled conversation in the background. Then Phyllis came on again. "Okay, where are you?"

"Across from Jackson Square, by the art store."

"Stay right where you are, don't move. I'll be there in half an hour."

When Phyllis pulled up in front of the art store, she had her boy-did-you-blow-it-this-time look on. She was still wearing her uniform from work. It made me think of the nurses at the hospital. I wondered how Grace was.

Bridget and I climbed into the backseat. I leaned against the side of the car and rested my feet on the hump in the floor. I hadn't realized until then how exhausted I was. I wondered if this was how Grace felt, lying in her hospital bed.

"Where do you two *get* these ideas?" Phyllis demanded, as she maneuvered through the rush-hour traffic. "This reminds me of the time Dad pulled you out of that crazy jazz funeral."

I shot Bridget a glance. She shook her head and laughed silently.

"Didn't you learn enough from that?" Phyllis persisted. "Don't you remember how mad Dad was?"

"Phyllis," I said, mustering all the patience I could, "this is not like the jazz funeral. We went shopping. We just lost track of time—"

"I'll say. Dad's been waiting an hour for you. He's mad, too. It's not that you went shopping, it's where you went. Twelve years old and traipsing around the French Quarter!"

"Oh, Phyllis, knock it off!" I said crossly. "If Dad's mad, let him tell me himself."

Phyllis clamped her mouth shut and drove on in silence.

We dropped Bridget off and then went home. Dad came storming out of the house as soon as the car pulled up. Sharon trailed out behind him. He flung open the car door. The vein in his forehead was jumping. "What do you mean by going to the French Quarter without permission?" he started.

My feet hurt. All I wanted to do was lie down or take a warm bath. I looked at him blankly.

"Haven't I told you it's no place for a young girl? Do you know what kind of people hang around down there?"

"People who make me happy," I said. "Which is more than what happens around here!"

"Look here, young lady," Dad returned. "I'm in no mood for sassing. You know you're expected to ask permission for things like this!"

I felt the heat rising to my face. "I hate it here!" I shouted. "I'm just like a prisoner." My eyes burned and suddenly I burst into tears. I sat down on the sidewalk, burying my face in my arm. Then I felt a hand on my shoulder. I looked up and it was Sharon. She gazed at me. I looked away.

Dad stood there, his arms dangling limply by his sides.

"It's more than this that's upset you, isn't it?" she asked gently.

I nodded.

"Are you worried about Grace?"

I nodded.

"Have you seen her lately?"

"Yes!" I shouted. "And she looks awful!" Then I ran into the house and locked myself in my room.

CHAPTER
9

Ten days later, Bridget left for the workshop. I was going to the train station with her, her mother and Brian to see her off. Brian was going to New York, too, not to the workshop, but to stay with a friend. He would ride up and back on the train with Bridget. I made a mental note to tell Dad that the Calloways were not so liberal; Bridget had a chaperone for the whole trip.

Brian just had a knapsack on his back, but Bridget had a knapsack and a suitcase in each hand. It was mostly art supplies and hats, I think.

I squeezed into the front seat with Bridget and Mrs. Calloway. The sudden change from the heat outside to the air-conditioned car gave me goose bumps. I leaned my head against the closed window and looked across Bridget at her mother. I liked watching Mrs. Calloway. She was an older version of Bridget. Her hair was soft and brown like Bridget's, only shoulder-length.

She didn't wear makeup. "People will have to take me the way the good Lord made me!" she said. She talked like that even though Bridget said she probably didn't believe in God. Today she was wearing two silver bracelets and silver earrings they had bought on an Indian reservation when they went out West last summer.

Brian, scrunched up in the backseat with a paperback called *Wilderness Survival* on his knees, didn't talk the whole ride to the station.

Bridget could scarcely contain herself, however. "Carrie, I wish you were going. I'll write down everything that happens, so you won't miss it completely."

I nodded. I was thinking of a kind of tiered shelf I'd seen once, wondering if I could construct it. It would be perfect in Grace's greenhouse. I could get it all built and painted, maybe take a picture of it to show to Grace. It would inspire her to get well.

Dimly, I was aware that Bridget was rambling on. "Mom," she said, "Uncle Greg said this workshop turned his whole view of art upside down."

"I'm glad you're excited," Mrs. Calloway said, smiling.

Bridget tilted her head and looked at me. "I should be quiet about this stuff. Carrie, you look so down. You must wish you were going now."

"No, it's okay. I'm just thinking." There was the problem of where to build it. I couldn't do it outside. It would take several days, and if it rained, the wood would warp. We had a small basement, but Dad had cleared that out for Sharon's sports stuff. She had an exercise bike and weights and all kinds of junk, Dad said.

Finally, we pulled up in front of the train station. It was loud and dirty. People wandered around, looking exhausted and lost. The announcements on the loud-speakers grated on my ears. We finally found the right train, and Bridget hugged and kissed us both good-bye. She and Brian boarded and took seats where we could see them. We stood watching until the train disap-peared. Bridget waved the whole time. Brian waved once and returned to his book. I was relieved that she was gone. I didn't want to talk about the workshop any-more.

Mrs. Calloway put her arm around me. "I have a little time for a snack before I go back to the office. Would you like to join me?" she asked.

"Sure."

Mrs. Calloway drove straight to the French Quar-ter and parked by Jackson Square. Leon was out on the Square with his paintings. I smiled and he nodded. As we walked over to the Café du Monde, I felt uneasy. I'd just gotten hollered at for being here. But I guessed this was different since I was with an adult.

The café was crowded, but finally a group left a small table on the outside. The sounds of the riverboats drifted up to us. I thought of stowing away and going out to sea to a deserted island somewhere. I'd eat fish and coconuts, and I wouldn't have to talk to anyone.

Mrs. Calloway touched my hand. "You're far away," she commented.

"I was just thinking."

"I'm sorry you weren't able to go with Bridget. It must have been very disappointing."

"It doesn't matter," I said.

"I understand that Mrs. Stebbins is in the hospital. She's a friend of yours, Bridget tells me."

"I'm about her best friend, I guess," I told her.

"And your father is getting married again soon, too."

"Yes'm. In September."

"That's a lot of changes. This must be a very difficult time for you."

I felt flustered. After a minute's silence I took a big bite of my doughnut. Powdered sugar puffed out like a cloud. "These doughnuts sure are messy."

Mrs. Calloway wasn't the only one who suddenly decided I needed some attention. Dad took me bowling one night and to the movies another. Phyllis and Al invited me to join them for a pizza. I guess the night I sat down on the sidewalk and cried worried them. Everybody probably got together and decided to keep my mind off things.

And then there was Sharon. Dad said, "Sharon's planning to ask you to help out at the store one night soon."

"Can't she afford to hire anybody?"

Dad's face was stamped with patience. "She thought it might be something different the two of you could do together."

"I thought people always went to the zoo in these situations," I said snidely.

"Carrie," Dad said, revealing a thin patch in his patience, "she is trying not to treat you as a child, but you'll have to be worthy of that treatment."

I placed my chin in one cupped hand and looked out the window. "Do I have to go?"

"I would like for you to go."

There was a square of silence where our separate wills locked horns and battled. Mine lost.

"Okay," I said. "I'll go."

The "invitation" came. Dutifully, I accepted it.

The Good Sports Shop had everything from sweatbands to archery targets. It was a big store and every inch of it was put to use. It was painted with several shades of yellow, beginning with a pale lemon color where the bats, balls, and other popular items were. The last band of color was a brilliant golden yellow that made the stacks of gray sweat clothes and school gym suits seem to pop out at you.

A whole bunch of gym suits had come in for the fall, and we worked together in the back of the store, pricing and stacking them.

I rued the weakness of my will. Sharon had me alone and trapped. I braced myself.

"You know," Sharon said, "sports sometimes do

surprising things for people. More than just building muscles and improving coordination."

"Oh."

"Yes. Sports can affect the way a person feels. The way he handles himself."

"I think sports are dumb."

Sharon stopped in the middle of writing out a price tag and looked at me. "How so?"

I made a face. "People chasing around after a ball like it was the most important thing in the world—seems like a waste of time."

She smiled. "There are a lot of people who get frustrated easily—or it seems that way. They bottle their feelings up. Then one day something happens, maybe something where they really need to be understanding. But they've already stretched their patience to the limit. So they blow up."

I felt Sharon's eyes on me and concentrated on folding gym suits. This was no random conversation. "So what's that got to do with sports?"

"Well, people can release their frustrations in sports, if they play regularly. Then they are more relaxed."

In the back, the air-conditioning unit rattled and began to hum.

"Your dad is that way, Carrie," Sharon continued. "He loves you a lot and he's anxious to understand you. But, sometimes, out of frustration, he goes barreling in, angry about one problem, totally missing a bigger one."

She allowed a thoughtful silence to fall. Sports was not the issue, of course. It was an excuse to talk about Dad and why he had yelled at me that evening. Sharon had understood. She'd known that I was really crying over Grace. Dad hadn't.

I broke open the last package of gym suits. "Looks like we're almost done," I said.

"Yes," said Sharon.

We were quiet on the way home, but not uncomfortably so. When we walked in the house, Dad bounced up from his easy chair, eager to know how we passed the time and so on. Sharon discreetly excused herself to the kitchen.

"How'd things go?" Dad asked for the third time.

"Okay," I said.

"What did you do?"

"Priced and put up gym suits."

Dad's square face was earnest and hopeful. "Did you *talk*?" he asked cautiously. "Do you feel like you know her better?"

More out of habit than meanness I searched for some shattering retort, but found none. It was getting hard to hate Sharon. "We talked some," I said simply.

Dad's brown eyes roved over my face for a moment and then he smiled and gave my shoulder a little shake. "That's great! That's really great, Carrie!"

I smiled wanly and watched him bound off toward the kitchen.

*   *   *

A couple of nights later, I had to go to a swim meet at the Y with them. They started toward the building arm in arm, and I drifted away from them. As if on a signal, they separated and were suddenly on either side of me, walking into the Y.

I couldn't get too excited about seeing people sloshing around in a swimming pool, knocking themselves out to be the first one to get to the other side. As long as you got where you're going, I didn't see what difference it made if you took five seconds or five minutes. But the top swimmers in various age groups from all over Louisiana were competing against each other, and Dad and Sharon were quite excited about it.

"Well, Carrie," Dad said. "This will be your first swim meet and your first time seeing people in serious competition. I haven't been to one myself since high school."

"Uh huh."

"Some of the people you see tonight could end up in the Olympics," Sharon said.

"Really?"

"Yes! Swimmers usually reach their peak at about fourteen or fifteen—not too much older than you."

The smell of chlorine was overpowering. The rippling water made the black lines on the bottom of the pool wriggle like snakes. The swimmers, sleek and tan, waited at the edge of the pool. They did warm-up exercises and talked softly among themselves.

Sharon offered Dad and me some gum, and I took

a stick. I was aware of a faint, nagging restlessness. I knew its name. Grace. I hadn't been to see her yesterday or today. I had seen her on Wednesday, and though she smiled and talked with me, she reminded me of a transplanted flower, curling its leaves downward in the sunshine. I came home depressed. Phyllis asked if Grace's condition was upsetting me.

"You can't keep going there every day. You need a break. This happens to nurses all the time. They call it burnout. Seeing sick people all the time gets them down, so they have to stay away for a while."

"But Grace doesn't get away. She's stuck there, feeling bad, every day," I argued. "I have to go. I'm her closest friend. She needs visits."

"Of course," said Phyllis rationally. "But if you're depressed, it will only make her feel worse. Believe me, Carrie, take off a day or so and you'll be much better for her. Grace will understand."

So I stayed away.

The loudspeaker buzzed. The swimmers raised their heads. "Ladies and gentlemen. Welcome to the annual YMCA Swim Meet. In the coed nine-year-old freestyle competition, we have, in lane one, Elizabeth Moncure from Gretna; lane two, Gerald Washington from Baton Rouge; lane three . . ." The swimmers took their places, a whistle blew and they dove.

The races seemed to be endless. There were races for different strokes and different age groups, all the way up through teen-age. The announcer labored over each swimmer's name and town, fighting to be heard over the static in the loudspeaker and the echo in the room. The loudspeaker reminded me of the one in the hospital.

Sharon sat on one side of me, pointing out what was good and bad about every swimmer and predicting winners. Most of the time, she was right. Dad, sitting on the other side, leaned toward her, listening.

"This is like being ringside with Howard Cosell," said Dad. "It means a lot more when you have someone here who knows the sport."

Once Sharon reached behind me to grab Dad's shoulder. "Watch the girl in lane three," she whispered to Dad and me. "That's really an exceptional stroke."

I leaned forward to separate myself from them. I looked around the audience, trying to get ideas for cartoons, but nothing came. At the pool, the seventeen-year-old girls were lining up for the butterfly competition. They all wore tight white caps and blue tank suits. The whistle blew and they dove as if shot from the concrete. Their arms flung out into a V in front of them, then, pushing the water down and away, they gasped quickly for air and buried their heads in water again. Over and over they flung and gasped, desperately struggling forward until I imagined all seven drowning before our eyes. Suddenly the white caps seemed like white hair and the swimmers became Grace, gasping desperately for air. My stomach knotted up. I pushed past Sharon and ran out into the night. I stood outside until I caught my breath. I glanced at my watch. Visiting hours at the hospital would soon be over, but I had to see Grace. If I hurried, I could probably make it. From where I stood, I could see part of the hospital, several blocks away.

I hadn't even gotten past the Y when a yellow hatchback pulled up beside me.

"Want a lift?" Sharon asked.

I hesitated. "Only if you're going to the hospital."

"Hop in."

We didn't speak on the way over. I didn't know where Dad was, but I supposed he took a cab home. When I got out, Sharon said, "I've been wanting to meet your friend Grace. Do you mind if I come along?"

I really did mind, but I couldn't very well say so. "I guess not."

Grace wasn't in her room. We went to the nurses' station to find out where she was. A nurse was busily arranging medicines on a tray.

"When will Mrs. Stebbins be back in her room?" I asked.

The nurse glanced up without really seeing me. "Mrs. Stebbins isn't here anymore. Transferred out today."

"She went home, you mean?"

Mrs. Du Bois leaned out of the medicine closet and, seeing me, hurried out. She laid a hand on my shoulder. "Carrie, dear, Mrs. Stebbins was transferred to a nursing home this afternoon. The decision was made just yesterday."

"Why? Why couldn't she just go home?"

"Honey, sometimes it's hard for older people to manage alone, especially after a heart attack. Mrs. Stebbins didn't recover her strength entirely."

"What home did she go to?" Sharon asked.

"Thornton Hill Nursing Home," said Mrs. Du Bois. "It's a good home. Bright and pleasant, with a wonderful staff."

"I know the place," Sharon said. "I had an uncle there."

"Can we go see her tonight?" I asked.

Mrs. Du Bois glanced at her watch. "Visiting hours are over for tonight. I believe they start again at ten A.M. tomorrow."

"We'll go tomorrow, Carrie," said Sharon. "First thing."

I started to say I'd get there myself, but suddenly I felt tired. I couldn't fight anymore.

We walked back out to the parking lot in silence. Just before we reached the car, Sharon put her arm around me.

"Carrie, you okay?"

"Yeah. I just wish I could go to sleep forever," I mumbled.

"I'm really sorry this has happened. I know you were counting on Grace coming home."

Tears sprang up in my eyes and I knew that to try to answer would be to set them loose. I bit my lip and did not cry.

CHAPTER
10

Sharon arrived promptly at nine-thirty on Saturday morning and didn't waste any time talking with Dad before leaving. Dad didn't ask any questions or praise me for going somewhere with Sharon.

The nursing home was in the suburbs, Sharon told me as we rumbled along. It would be about a half-hour drive.

It was perfect weather. The heat was softened by an easy breeze, but I found myself hating the day. I felt as if I was in a fog. "Sharon, what happened to your uncle?" I asked. "The one who was in this nursing home."

"He died some years ago."

A wave of grayness rolled over me.

Sharon glanced at me. "Carrie, not everyone dies in nursing homes. Sometimes they get better and can go on to special apartments for the elderly. Sometimes they even go home."

Thornton Hill Nursing Home was a low, U-shaped building at the crest of a slight rise in the land. There were trees, and a walkway lined with flowers.

We went into a lobby where several old people were sitting, talking with visitors. At the nurses' station, we were told that Grace was in the East Wing, Room 4, Bed B.

"I'll wait here, if you'd like to visit with Grace alone," Sharon offered.

"Okay," I said. "Thanks."

I walked down the hall with my hands in my pockets. An old woman with a walker passed me.

The first bed in Grace's room was empty. Grace was sitting in a red vinyl chair by her bed, looking out the window. A yellow sweater was draped around her shoulders.

"Grace?" I said tentatively.

She turned in her chair and smiled. Her eyes were very sad. "Carrie, how nice of you to come," she said.

"I went to the hospital last night, but you had already gone. And the day before—well, I'm sorry I didn't come."

"It's all right. You were my most faithful visitor. I didn't expect you to come every day."

I stood there, reaching for words.

"Do come and sit down," said Grace. "I haven't a chair for you, but there's the bed."

I sat down on the edge of the bed and immediately

felt uncomfortable. It put me above her. She was dwarfed by the chair.

"Life seems to have taken yet another turn," she said.

"I don't understand!" I burst out. "Why are you here? When are you coming home?"

Grace reached out and touched my hand. "Carrie, the future is uncertain. The doctors, my sister, they thought it best that I be where there are others around . . . where I won't work so hard."

"But you were doing fine at home. I could come over every day, even after school. I'll help with the chores."

She shook her head. "I know you would, Carrie, and you're wonderful to offer. I was fortunate with this heart attack. I felt the pains and was able to call the ambulance. Mrs. Goldstein, my roommate, fell and broke her hip. She lay on her apartment floor a day and a half before someone found her."

I had no answer for that. If Grace fell in the night, and I didn't come until after school . . . If she had a second heart attack, but couldn't make it to the phone . . .

I followed Grace's eyes out the window to where the green leaves stood motionless in the bright sky. There was an expanse of lawn; I wished I could run across it until the sadness was all gone. "Soon you'll get your strength back," I said. "Then you'll come home."

"Perhaps to an apartment. My sister is putting the

house up for sale. It's very expensive to stay here. I can't afford to keep the house—and it seems to be too much work for me, in any case." She ran her hand along the smooth, shiny surface of her chair. "They were right, of course, to send me here," she said softly. "I'm just sorry, so very sorry, that they were."

She saw my face and smiled again. "Carrie, perhaps I will move to an apartment not far from you. You'll visit, and we'll sit out on the balcony. Or perhaps walk to a corner café for lemonade."

She closed her eyes and breathed deeply. As I watched her, she seemed to be drawing in strength. Then she opened her eyes and smiled like her old self. I felt something lighten inside of me. "I seem to be behaving like a foolish old woman again," she said. She rose and put her hands on my shoulders. "Carrie, life doesn't always give us what we want. Sometimes it gives us good times, sometimes difficulties and sorrow. We smile and say yes to it either way. Even though it may take us a moment to work up to that smile."

She turned to the dresser and began brushing her hair. "How did you come here today, Carrie? Did your father bring you?"

"No. Sharon did. She's waiting in the lobby."

"I'd like to meet her. Would you mind?"

"No. I don't mind."

We walked out to the lobby arm in arm and Sharon rose to greet us. "Mrs. Stebbins, I'm very glad to meet you. How are you feeling?"

"Much better, really, thank you. And please, call me Grace. Let's take a short walk, if you have the time." She gave my arm a little squeeze. "As Carrie knows, I'm not one to stay inside, and the day looks wonderful."

We made our way slowly down the walkway, Grace holding my arm to steady herself. She stopped midway, and we all sat down on a bench. On the other side of the walk, marigolds stood at measured distances like little orange-capped spikes.

"This garden is so sparse," Grace said, "don't you think?"

I nodded. "Yours is lots nicer."

"I promised the doctors I would rest, but as soon as I'm stronger, I'm going to find myself a trowel and make this a regular showplace!"

I smiled. "I'll come help!"

"You let us know when you're ready, Grace," said Sharon. "I'll get some flats of flowers. Just put in your order."

"Wonderful."

The next day a moving van came to Grace's house. I sat in my kitchen, swilling lemonade around in my glass, watching the men carry Grace's things out. What would Mrs. Appleby do with them? Stick them in her attic? Have a yard sale? Even if Grace got her own apartment one day, she'd never have room for everything.

The familiar sense of loss swept through me. Alone

in my room, I had finally cried last night, watching the shadows creeping over my walls. I picked up a postcard I had received from Bridget and stared blankly at the interior of a workshop classroom pictured on it. Bridget was learning and having fun and didn't know what had happened here. She got to travel a lot and was allowed to do all sorts of interesting things, but I was the one who went through all the big changes. It made me feel older somehow.

Outside, Mrs. Appleby ran out of the house and spoke to a moving man, who nodded in a bored way. Then she ran back in. In a moment, she was out again, chewing the ear off another mover. She wasn't cool and unruffled like Grace. I put my lemonade back in the refrigerator and went over.

I sat on the grass in front of the yard and watched. Then I called to Mrs. Appleby, offering to help.

"Thank you, child," she said, "but these men will take care of it. That's what they're paid for."

"Do you mind if I come in, then?" I was surprised at myself for asking, but it was my last chance to be in Grace's house.

Mrs. Appleby looked distracted. "Say there, those are vases in that box," she called to a moving man. "Please be careful." She glanced at me. "Come on in, honey. There's a pitcher of lemonade in the refrigerator and a few glasses in the cupboard."

I went into the kitchen and opened up the freezer. There were two frosted glasses there. They had roses on them. In the refrigerator were a couple of peaches, a package of cheese, and a big pitcher of lemonade.

I watched the packing and moving from the kitchen doorway. Grace's greenhouse was being pulled apart; she hadn't even had a chance to finish it. It made me feel awful.

The whole house was a mess, all the rooms half pulled apart. It was a nice little house. I supposed someone would come along and buy it quickly, someone who didn't care about flowers and who would let the garden die. They'd have little kids and would put up a swing set and a plastic wading pool in the yard and soon the grass would be trampled. Inside, the shelves would probably be cluttered with pictures of freckle-faced kids smiling into the camera or hiding behind their hands.

In the greenhouse, Grace's wedding picture was still hanging on the wall. I took it down and went back to the kitchen to look at it.

Mrs. Appleby came in and sat down, fanning herself with Grace's straw hat. "It surely is hot, it surely is."

"Would you like some lemonade, ma'am?"

"Well, now, that does sound mighty nice," she said. "I left it there to quench my thirst but haven't taken the time to have any."

I got the other rose glass from the freezer and poured her some lemonade. "Well, now, isn't that an idea," she said, when she saw the frosted glass. "I'd forgotten to check the freezer."

"What will happen to Mrs. Stebbins's things?" I asked.

"Well, she's asked for a few small items, which I'll take to her before I leave. Most of the rest will go into storage." She saw the picture on the table. "What have you got there, child?"

I showed her the picture of Grace and Edward. She sighed deeply. "Dear, dear Edward. He was a gentleman. My Grace has certainly had a share of troubles these late years. I don't know how she stood it when that man died, I surely don't."

"Grace—she asked me to call her that—Grace said we have to be ready to meet the new day. We have to go on."

Mrs. Appleby blinked at me. She touched her blue curls gingerly. For a moment we sat there looking at each other. Then Mrs. Appleby dabbed her mouth primly with her handkerchief. "That's all very well," she said, "but a relationship such as theirs was so close. You couldn't understand the grief, dear."

"Yes I could," I said hurriedly. "My mother died, so I know. Grace and I talked about it. You feel you want to give up, but you can't. Otherwise you might as well have died, too. It starts to get a little easier, even though you hate it. But you don't ever lose that person. Not really . . ."

My words trailed off and I looked at Grace's torn-up, half-packed house. Suddenly I realized that it didn't matter that Grace didn't get to finish the greenhouse.

Starting it was the important thing. It didn't even matter what you did exactly. How you lived was what counted. That was the real memorial—the way Grace kept getting up, doing her best.

I smiled suddenly at Mrs. Appleby, handed her the picture and started out of the house. Then I stopped. "Mrs. Appleby," I called. "Do you mind if I take some of these bachelor buttons along the walkway?"

"Help yourself, honey," she said. "They can't be packed."

I found a couple of big pots, dug the flowers up the way Grace had showed me and put them in the pots.

When I got home, Sharon was in the kitchen making dinner again. I put one pot in my room and one on the dining-room table.

"These are from Grace's garden," I announced. "I helped her plant them."

Sharon smiled. And, for the first time, I smiled back.

CHAPTER
11

The next day Al had a long talk with Dad, most of which I could hear by sitting quietly in my bedroom doorway. Al said he loved Phyllis and wanted to marry her, but he couldn't put her through nursing school and go to dental school at the same time. Dad said he and Phyllis had worked out a plan some time ago for helping her through school. If she would work part time during school and full time when school was out, he would still help her pay for the rest. He said he'd be proud to have Al for a son-in-law.

A day later, Phyllis announced that she and Al would get married during the spring break. This urge to get married must be an epidemic, I thought, and laughed.

Now Phyllis was showing Sharon pictures of silverware patterns and wedding dresses she liked. Once Phyllis handed Sharon a fat book of wedding dress pictures. "Is your dress in here, Sharon?" she asked.

"No, I'm not wearing a traditional wedding dress, Phyllis. Just a long, simple Indian one."

Phyllis looked shocked. "But what will they think at the church?"

"Well, actually, your dad and I have selected a small meeting hall. It's very nice, with trees all around. We're only inviting family, you know."

"Oh," said Phyllis, and left the room.

Sharon stood still for a moment, as if she was trying to decide whether to go after Phyllis.

"Don't worry about her, she'll get over it," I assured her. "Phyllis doesn't understand that people have to do things their own way. I think your wedding sounds neat."

Sharon looked at me and smiled.

"I was planning to have a lot of flowers at the wedding," she said tentatively. "Maybe you could help me select them at the florist's. Then we'll tell Phyllis and maybe that will cheer her up."

"Okay," I said.

During the next few days all of Grace's things were hauled away somewhere, a FOR SALE sign went up in the front yard and Mrs. Appleby returned to wherever she came from. I walked by to look at the garden. The weeds were starting to take over again. The bachelor buttons on the walkway had gotten so tall and bushy that they were leaning over across the path.

Then I heard a soft mewing. I looked up in the old

oak tree and there was Carrot. The basket and ladder were gone. Carrot mewed again and stood up on the branch. His orange tail swished back and forth. Suddenly he leaped to a lower branch. He stood there and blinked at me. Then he eased himself down the thick trunk, his long claws splayed out on the bark. In a moment, he was down. He swished his tail again, jumped into my arms and purred.

"Well," I said. "You did it. You're not scared of that old oak tree anymore!"

I took Carrot home and gave him a dish of milk and tuna fish.

"If you feed that cat here, he's just going to keep coming around," warned Phyllis.

"That's good," I said, " 'cause this is his new home until Grace is ready to take care of him."

"Oh, Carrie. I hate cats. They're always jumping up on furniture and scratching everybody."

"You don't know this cat," I said.

Phyllis shook her head and walked away.

On the evening of Bridget and Brian's return their parents were both tied up in meetings, so Dad and I went to the station to meet then. I could hardly wait to see Bridget. There were only a few days left before school started, but there was time for picnics and walks through the park and catching up.

Their train was on time, and we didn't have any trouble finding them. As soon as I saw a tall purple hat bobbing down the train steps, I knew it was Bridget.

Bridget and I squeezed up front with Dad, leaving Brian in the back. Brian was just the same as when he left. He said hello and pulled out a book called *Foraging for Food*.

Besides a hat, Bridget wore long gold earrings that jangled when she talked. She hardly stopped talking the whole trip back.

"Carrie, I tried things I hadn't even thought of at that workshop," she said. "There turned out to be a lot of introductory craft classes. Jewelry making, pottery—wait till you see the bowls I brought back. There just wasn't time to do all I wanted."

"How was New York?"

"Terrific. But too much to see." She pushed her long hair behind her ears. Her earrings quivered. "Uncle Greg says I better spend more time next year."

"You're going again?"

"I don't know. The workshop was so successful they're thinking of starting one in the South next summer."

"Really? Where?"

"Probably near Atlanta. Roy—he was my metal-sculpture instructor—will probably organize it. I really liked metal sculpture, so I might want to go there."

"Dad, Atlanta's not so far."

"It's worth looking into," he said.

"I've saved some of the money, and if I keep working through the school year—"

"Let me talk with Sharon," he said. "You know, we'll have two incomes starting in September."

Bridget gave me a quick look, and I grinned to let her know things were okay.

We pulled up in front of the Calloways' house. Dad handed Bridget a wedding invitation. "We hope you can come." He said it like he really meant it.